IN MY FATHER'S HOUSE

In My Father's House

TALES OF AN UNCONFORMABLE MAN

Nancy Huddleston Packer

JOHN DANIEL PUBLISHER · SANTA BARBARA · 1988

"Giving, Getting" and "The Man Who Hated Cigarettes" were first published in *The Reporter* (1964, 1968); "The Man Who Loved the Scenery" was first published in *Women's Studies* (1975); "Lee's Lieutenants" was first published in *Southern Humanities Review*; "The Man Who Said No" was first published in *Virginia Quarterly*, 1988; "Conversion and After" was first published in *Kenyon Review*, Vol. 30, No. 5, copyright ©1968 by Kenyon College (reprinted with permission of the *Kenyon Review*).

Designed and typeset in Garamond by Jim Cook
SANTA BARBARA, CALIFORNIA

LIBRARY OF CONGRESS CATALOGING IN PUBLICATION DATA
Packer, Nancy Huddleston.
In my father's house: tales of an unconformable man / Nancy Huddleston Packer.
ISBN 0-936784-34-2
1. Huddleston, George — Family. 2. Legislators — United States — Biography.
3. United States. Congress. House — Biography. 4. Packer. Nancy Huddleston —
Biography — Family. 5. Authors, American — 20th century — Biography —
Family. 6. Alabama — Biography.
I. Title.
E748.H82P33 1988
328.73′092′4—dc19   87-30470 CIP

Published by
JOHN DANIEL, PUBLISHER
Post Office Box 21922
Santa Barbara, California 93121

In memory of George and Bertha Huddleston

Contents

Giving, Getting 9

The Man Who Loved the Scenery 17

Lee's Lieutenants 28

The Man Who Hated Cigarettes 37

Conversion and After 47

The Birthday Party 58

The Man Who Said No 67

Giving, Getting

EARLY MEMORIES ARE CLOUDY, and often I can't separate myself from the other children in our family. Was it one of my sisters or I who cried when the Bonus Marchers came to Washington? Did all five of us march through Union Station bearing placards that said, Be Kind to Dumb Animals—Pity Hoover the Elephant? I'm not really sure. But I see myself separately and unmistakably Christmas of 1931, when I was six, for the story has been preserved intact in the annals of the family.

In good times and bad, we were a frugal family. My father was a member of Congress from Alabama and though the pay was not "handsome" (the Congress had voted itself a decrease in pay from $10,000 to $9,000 after, I venture to say, a roll call vote), we considered ourselves comfortably off. Re-election expenses surely totaled no more than a hundred dollars or so for gasoline my father used to travel the country roads and twenty-five dollars for printing up the cards he distributed. We had plenty, but nonetheless we took money seriously. Allowances and cash gifts were not bestowed merely to provide pleasure: they carried with them a test of virtue and a means to family standing.

Being the youngest, I was the last to be given any money. My

Saturday movie dime was entrusted to my brother George. As if poverty had made me mute, the ice cream man would ask my sister Jane what flavor I wanted. But that Christmas, everything changed.

On the Friday evening before the big day, my father called his children to him to dole out the Christmas spending money. He had not married until he was forty-eight but then had spawned a large family. He was a stern, just man, affectionate, but rather remote. His word was law in our house.

That evening, he gave each of my four brothers and sisters two dollars and fifty cents. After a slow appraising gaze, he took out two more dollars and a fifty cent piece and gave them to me. For a moment no one spoke. The older children exchanged glances. In a querulous voice that held no hope of prevailing, one of my sisters said,

"Nancy hasn't got two dollars and fifty cents worth of friends. The rest of us, like me. . ."

My father said, "Hush." Then he smiled at her. "There's no halfway house to equality. Nancy is equal now."

My brother George was five years older than I and very careful with money. He owned a little file case in which he kept a stack of I.O.U.s signed by his friends and family. When all of us went, say, to an amusement park, he chose his rides on the closely calculated basis of ride time to money. And so it was to him I went for advice on how to plan my Christmas spending.

"First you make a list," he said. He would do it for me since I couldn't really write. "Now you figure out how much you spend on everybody by how much you like them."

We commenced. By means of a private logic I can no longer recall, I settled on thirty-five cents for my mother and thirty for my father. Next came my brothers and sisters: Mary, George, John, and Jane. I directed George to write twenty cents beside each name.

"Everyone exactly the same, huh?" he said. "Okay, what about Ida?"

Instinctively I read his meaning. If I cared no more for him than for the others, then he would make it tough for me. "I reckon you didn't even think about Ida," he said harshly. "Poor as she is, much as she loves you."

Ida was our cook and was very important to all of us, but I hadn't thought I would buy her a present, for our parents gave her a nice one

10

from all of us. Nevertheless I fell before George's attack and said, "Twenty-five cents for Ida."

George stared at me but I was determined to hold my ground. "Twenty-five cents," I repeated. "How much have I got left?"

Grudgingly he informed me that I had eighty cents left. I directed him to write down ten cents beside the names of three school friends. That left Walter.

Walter lived next door and he was my hero. He was a year and a half older than I, the only child of a gay young larking couple. If we took pride in the penny saved, they took pleasure in the penny spent. Walter, who was not at all musical, had a grand piano, a trumpet in a leather case lined with blue velvet, and a real kettledrum.

"Forty cents for Walter," I said.

"You're even stupider than I thought," George said. "You won't have but a dime left for yourself." I ignored for the moment what this disclosed of George's plans for his own two dollars and fifty cents. I was too pleased with the windfall.

In addition to the traits I've mentioned, my father was eccentric. Much that he did caused his children that peculiar double pain of embarrassment and shame for being embarrassed. We cringed doubly on the snowy afternoon when he walked home from the House Office Building with newspapers wrapped around his legs to protect his trousers. We were humiliated when he started the car and to save gas shifted to high gear so fast that the car bucked for two blocks. When he decided on the spur of the moment to take us to do our shopping that Christmas Eve, we understood that his presence conferred an honor upon us. But beneath our false glad cries when he told us he would accompany us lurked the miserable self-consciousness of inveterate criminals about to be sentenced to the pillory.

Our father had not taken his daily walk, and so we walked to the nearest shopping area eight blocks away. Woolworth's was teeming with children, and not even our father's magnificent will would be able to hold us in a band. Quickly he calculated aptitudes and dispositions, paired and totaled them, and sent us out like snipers to distant corners. I was sent with George, who of course would not pursue his own pleasure in buying until he had exhausted mine.

Setting off at a dogtrot, round and round the store we went. At last

11

we landed at Glassware. We were always breaking glasses, George insisted, wanting to get me started. My eye was caught by a set of thick blue glasses set in holes cut in a tin tray.

"It says brandy glasses," said George. "That's liquor."

"Mother doesn't drink brandy," I said.

"Look," he said impatiently, "she has a lot of flower vases, hasn't she? Does that mean she drinks flower water? Get 'em."

I got them. Thirty-five cents. It was quite a moment, but George would not let me enjoy it to the full. He hurried me off to the necktie counter. On my own I selected a red-and-yellow necktie for my father to replace the black bow tie he always wore. There was a slight hitch: the tie only cost twenty-nine cents.

"You're only cheating him by a penny," said George.

"I could put the penny in the package," I said.

"If you want to," he said, "stupid."

Ida was more of a problem. I knew nothing of her life outside our house. She did have boy friends, tall, kindly dark men who came to sit with her when she stayed with us those rare evenings when our parents went out. How did they entertain themselves, I often wondered, once the floor show had gone to bed? I bought a deck of playing cards for a quarter to tide them through their boredom in our absence.

We had circled the store many times, and George's impatience was growing. We were between Drugs and Toys and he kept trying to work me over to Toys. I would not be worked. In a sudden huff, he told me to go to hell and vanished. At once he returned, looking both vicious and contrite.

"If he found out I left you. . . ."

"I promise I won't tell him."

After a searching look, he decided to trust me. He departed and I turned at once not to Toys but to Drugs. My brothers were only seventeen months apart and each measured his worth by the other. For the sake of peace, everyone gave them the same presents. I knew what I wanted to buy for them because I knew what they wanted. Our eldest sister, Mary, fastidious to a fault, had a large bottle of Lavoris mouthwash that was the envy of us all. It was red and flavorful and mysterious, and we stole swigs from the bottle. Not a week before, my brother John had been caught with the bottle at his lips. With his customary bravado, he had said, "It ain't nearly as good as Listerine." I bought John and George each a twenty-cent bottle of Listerine.

Too timid to leave that section of the store alone and victimized by impulse, I quickly bought vanishing cream and powdered rouge for my sisters and a bottle of blood-red fingernail polish for my three school friends. These were exactly the kinds of selections my father had expected George to prevent. But they cleared the way for the big moment: Walter's present.

Poor Walter was always deprived by excess. When the other boys played football, they wore gray sweatshirts and dirty blue jeans and Keds. When Walter joined them, he wore padded pants that forced him to goose-step, regulation shoulder pads that held his arms spread-eagled, and an immense helmet that crashed down across his vision at the moment of impact. He looked like Frankenstein's monster. And while the rest of us had pistols into which we inserted single torn-off caps, Walter had a repeater machine gun that consumed a roll of caps before he could get his finger off the trigger or his eye on the target. Recently he had tried to swap his expensive gun for a cheap one, but his desperation had spoiled everything and no one would swap. I wanted to please him, and I had decided to get him a pistol.

The ordinary cap pistol cost twenty cents, and so I bought two, to use up the forty cents. I gave the saleswoman my fifty cent piece, which was all I had left except for the awkward penny from my father's present. She gave me a sack containing the two pistols and some coins which I dropped into my coat pocket. As I stood there, I had the vague feeling that the coins amounted to more than the dime George had said I would have left. I went in search of advice.

Pushing and squeezing past adult backsides and children's shoulders, I wriggled my way through the store after George and found him paying for a large bottle of perfume. "How much is this?" I said, holding out my coins.

At that precise moment, the thundering voice of our father crashed down upon us. He was stationed at the front of the store ready to go home, and he was summoning us in the most efficacious manner he knew. Oblivious of our pain, our shameful pain, in his booming orator's voice and in chronological order he called us to him. At once the entire store went silent.

"Mary!" he shouted. A slight reverberating pause. I imagined her collapsing in a heap across the pots and pans. "George!" George chewed his tongue, winced, cast darting glances right and left, cornered, little, quick. "John!" Cool, nonchalant, John would pretend to ignore the voice, would idly finger the goods, and then race to answer the summons. "Jane!" Jane had no doubt found a friend to whom she gave a glance that said, "Jane who?" She knew. "Nancy!" he shouted. I was too young to know how humiliated I was, but I whimpered because I wanted to be like the older children.

We walked home in the cold, through the cold streets, clutching our packages and our pain, no one daring to complain, no one old enough to laugh. Our father asked if we had had a successful trip. Oh yes, we murmured. When we got home, Mary burst into the house, shot Mother an I-told-you-it-would-be-awful look, and rushed to her room.

"What's wrong with her?" my father asked. Mother knew but she said nothing. There was no point going into it, for that would have brought forth from our father a lecture on false pride. We recovered at speeds becoming to our ages. I recovered most quickly, having my money still in mind. I went in search of George.

"I gave her a fifty cent piece," I said, showing him the coins, "and she gave me this."

"That's sixty cents," he said. He looked at me with incredulity and admiration. "You pulled a fast one, kid, you rooked 'em good. You're not so stupid after all."

Oh, but I was. Ignoring my brother's entreaties, beaming with pride, confident at last of status and praise, I went sailing back to my father. "They gave me too much change," I said. My halo fairly glittered.

Without the slightest show of response, for he had an infinite capacity for patience, he asked me to tell him exactly what I had bought and how much I had paid. I produced my dog-eared list and my purchases so he could see the prices. When he had carefully examined the sales slips, he said, "Get your coat and bring that money."

By the time I had absorbed the full import of that, the news had flashed through the house. My brothers and sisters gathered behind the banisters, silently mocking me. What a dolt. What a simp.

Although their epithets were mouthed or whispered, so my father wouldn't catch them, I began to cry. I knew they were right.

"Honor," my father said as he closed the front door. "Honesty," he said as we walked down the walk to the car. "Fair dealing." We got in the car. "Honor. Honesty. Fair dealing," he repeated as he started the car. "These are virtues without which civilization cannot endure. Money," he went on as we bucked down the street and headed toward Woolworth's, "is one of the great threats to virtue. Beware of it. Let this be an abiding lesson to you."

By next morning, my brothers and sisters had forgotten me in the thrill of Christmas. Everyone liked my presents except my brothers. It turned out that they were not as fond of Listerine as I had thought. In fact, only after they found out that I had two cap pistols for Walter would they speak to me. Then they berated, cajoled, wheedled, nagged, begged, and ultimately persuaded me to exchange their presents for Walter's. They went roaring through the house shooting caps while I rewrapped the Listerine in fancy paper.

I had barely finished when Walter and his mother came knocking at our door. Walter had on a new baseball uniform with regulation shoes. He walked quite carefully across the floor. He had a large package for me, wrapped in navy-blue paper and tied with a gold ribbon. His mother was all smiles and elegance as she watched him give it to me.

"If it doesn't fit," she told my mother, "do exchange it."

It was a baby-blue sweater with a white angora yoke. My mother flushed and coughed and looked hopeless. "It's lovely," she said. "You shouldn't have."

With flamboyance and pride—for I had chosen everything all by myself—I gave Walter his present. He felt, smelled, licked the package, and when he shook it and heard the faint gurgle, he began to dance a little jig of excitement on his cleats. No doubt he thought it was whiskey. Bits of paper and ribbon flew about the room. And then dead silence fell among us. Walter held in each hand a bottle of Listerine. Though I had bought the Listerine, made the swap for the pistols, wrapped the package, I recoiled with shock.

"Well, Nancy," said his mother, "two bottles of Listerine. I'm sure Walter can take that big a hint."

She was laughing, of course, and my mother was laughing. But

Walter was not laughing. With a whoop of rage, he threw the bottles onto the sofa where I was sitting, holding the sweater, and on his spikes went screeching, sliding, cutting, tearing out of the living room and out of the house. His mother was in close pursuit.

Attracted by all the commotion, my father came to the doorway. When he saw me, he said, "Well, Nanny, how do you like being a full-fledged participant in the yearly giving and getting? What's your verdict?" He smiled tenderly.

I could not answer him then, and I'm not sure I could now. I still make my list and by the secret scale of love decide approximately how much for whom. During the course of the buying, I deceive myself and others. And on Christmas night, as certain as the season, after all the presents have been exchanged and the disappointments duly felt and recorded along with the rare perfect success, then I ask myself why giving and getting, these simple pleasures, end so often in comic failure.

The Man Who Loved the Scenery

IN 1931 WE TRADED in the tin lizzie touring car, which was classy looking but rickety and unreliable, on a brand new Chevrolet. After that, every summer our family drove back and forth the 850 miles between Washington and Birmingham.

On every one of these trips, we suffered at least a minor catastrophe. We broke a rear axle in Valdosta, we sideswiped a Plymouth and bounced against a telephone pole near Kingsport, we got lost for hours on a dirt road shortcut outside Greensboro. As we drove along, most of us in the car girded ourselves for disaster. But until it struck, my father enjoyed his most lighthearted moments of the year. These trips—ordeals for the rest of us—were as close as he ever came to a vacation.

He was hard-working and serious-minded and did not indulge the Washington cocktail circuit, if there was one then, did not attend embassy parties, if he was ever invited, scarcely missed a roll call vote in his twenty-two years in the House, and spent his evenings and Sundays on pending legislation. He was slight and quick and powerful, unharmed by whiskey or tobacco and strengthened by an innate austerity, a spartan regime that included cold showers in the morning, and five young children.

We were a rowdy bunch, full of noise and fight, but he never punished us. He never had to. When he gave a signal—a muted sound in his throat, a name spoken quietly—free-for-alls stopped in mid-punch, raucous laughter abruptly died. He was, simply, an awesome presence for us. Except, that is, on these trips up and down the Eastern Seaboard, when he became as easy and gay as the young fathers of our friends.

He was a terrible driver. He had come late to the automobile and he treated it as if it needed no more attention than an old horse moving along under a loose rein. In his lifetime he must have had a dozen wrecks, though none serious. He passed on hills and curves, he took his half in the middle, he challenged at every crossing.

Mostly he watched the scenery. Whipping by a truckload of lumber, he watched heavy clouds shifting and forming. Rounding a hairpin turn, he caught sight of a scurrying animal and let his eyes chase it to its burrow. He delighted in every bush and mountain and stream he saw. And he saw them all, his touch light on the steering wheel, his foot heavy on the gas.

My mother hated the trips as much as he liked them. She was much younger than he and generally full of respect, even awe. But when he was at the wheel of a car, she thought he was a reckless, incompetent fool. As he watched the scenery, she watched the road. She ground her fists in her lap. She slammed her foot into the floorboard with such vigor that by the time we arrived at our destination, the seat of her dress was in shreds.

She was only casually religious, but half her words were supplications to the deity for help and safety. The other half was used to beg, cajole, accuse my father. Slow down! Dear God! You'll kill us all! Lord help us! How much of this was exaggerated, I never knew. It may be she used this opportunity of his incompetence and lightheartedness to express serious complaints she otherwise tried to repress.

When my father wasn't looking at the scenery, he was looking at her, enjoying her outrage. They were more aware of each other during these trips than ever at home. They were constantly at each other with the teasing play that must have marked their courtship. All in good fun, I guess, but as their spirits rose, we children grew more and more apprehensive, because sometimes the hostility won out over the good humor, and then we would all be in for it.

18

On a bright, clear June day in 1933, we set out for Birmingham by way of the Blue Ridge Mountains of Virginia. My mother must have felt she was going on a honeymoon in Hell. She was afraid of all high places, especially mountains. Even in her eighties, as we swooped up a six-lane freeway over the Santa Cruz Mountains, she cleared her throat—that warning sound I've recognized as long as I've known any symbol—and I slowed down. She didn't have to go on the trip over the Blue Ridge, of course. She could have taken the train. But under the perhaps specious guise of protecting her children or of taking over the driving if my father got sick, she went that time, too. Maybe she wanted to be there when the big catastrophe struck so she could point out what bad judgment he had. Or maybe she just wanted to savor, though at cost to herself, his only carefree moments. Maybe a honeymoon in Hell was better than no honeymoon at all.

My father roused us out of bed at 5:30. "Bristol by nightfall," he explained. He began to arrange our suitcases in the small trunk of the Chevy and the rest of our gear on the outside, great canvas sacks lashed on with clothesline every which of a way, stuck down alongside the spare tire set in the fender, escaping out of the trunk, tied on the roof and overhanging the windows, until the car looked like the soft belly of a giant creased by a belt.

The younger children didn't mind; we liked people staring after us. But Mary, who was fourteen, was furious to tears. She declaimed, only to our mother, that it was surely not absolutely essential that we ride through the countryside looking so scrubby. And of course she knew it was deliberate: our father did it to humiliate her. Couldn't Mother do anything? The families of other congressmen managed to appear respectable somehow. They shipped their belongings ahead, didn't carry their entire household possessions on the *roof*. Some of them had drivers, some traveled by train, some had two cars so people had room for their feet, or maybe they didn't have to have so many children, maybe they at least left their dog at home.

"Other people," said Mary, "have the decency not to look like hoboes."

"Other people," Mother said, "are not your father. Your father," she said putting the responsibility for him squarely on us, "doesn't like side."

19

That's pretentious, he often said, just phony. If we gagged at a dish of brains-and-eggs, he told us to quit posturing. If we begged not to wear long underwear because no other children had to wear it, he said we were just indulging in side. We knew he was right, and we were ashamed. But we were not consoled.

Mary spent the last half hour in front of her mirror, practicing looks of disdain she would never cast at him, rehearsing lines of rebellion she would never utter. We were a teasing bunch and as we marched by her room we sent shafts of wit into her: What has more side than one Mary? Two Marys. We sang: Oh Mary's going to Alabama with dirty laundry on her knee, she comes from Washington for everyone to see. . . .

Mother said, "Don't tease her. Some day you'll understand."

And she was right. Every year another of us understood. Come to that humorless age, quick to feel shame, filled with rebellion and self-absorption, like Mary we tried to insulate ourselves from the family. We hid too long upstairs to avoid the amused glances of the milkman or a dog-walker. And we paid for it, as she did that day.

We were down on the sidewalk, ready to leave, everyone but Mary. My father had an orator's voice that seemed to carry miles, deep, resonant, penetrating. He called into the stillness of the morning, "All aboard, Mary." Thus were the neighbors—girls she admired, boys she hoped admired her—aroused from their sleep in the nick of time to see Mary desperately cinching up a little sack of her things. The wages of side.

All the other children jumped for the car, shoving and clawing for the window seats, until my father established a fair rotation. There were a lot of people in that car: four of the five children (my lucky sister Jane was to come down two days later with my father's secretary), our parents, and Ida Moore who worked for us. Also our dog.

Duke was half Great Dane and half German Shepherd. He easily could and often did jump our four-foot fence to chase anything on wheels. Policemen patrolled on bicycles in Washington in those days, and one trigger-happy cop gave Duke a bullet hole from his neck through his shanks. Duke survived and became a neighborhood hero. Although I still don't understand why we allowed him to terrorize bicyclists, I remember him as a loving and gentle dog. We used to saddle him with an old quilt and bridle him with string, and then we'd sell dogback rides for a cent apiece. Duke would get about halfway to the corner, trotting nicely, when he would catch sight of a cat and would take off. He left the rider sprawled on the concrete, weeping, bleeding, bilked.

Duke took his place on the floor of the backseat, stretched from window to window, already panting and slobbering as we drove out of the city. The wind that cooled him whipped strings of his spit into our faces. After we had slowed down for Anacostia and speeded up again, he lunged between two of us onto the back seat so he could stare sullenly out the back window. We howled and shoved him, and soon war broke out.

My father said, "Duke," in that muted voice of his. Duke was a true Huddleston child. No one could do anything with any of us except my father, and he could do whatever he wanted. Duke meekly returned to the floor. My father dropped his hand over the back of the front seat and scratched Duke's ear.

"Guide with both hands," my mother cried. She was sitting in the front, with my brother George in the middle. "Oh God, there's a car. Look out."

"Where? Where? I can't see a thing." My father roared out his first laugh of the trip. All of us, except Mother, laughed, even Ida Moore.

Mother said, "Laugh, clowns, laugh," her customary response when the joke was on her.

Ida stared out the window. She could take herself right out of that car any time she wanted to. She was a handsome, high-cheeked black woman with a narrow chin and large white teeth and lots of boy friends. Mother always said Ida went with us to Alabama every summer in order to cut loose the current boy friend so she could start fresh when she returned in the autumn. And it was true that she was hedonistic, clear-eyed, and philosophic. This became apparent to us when she refused to move permanently to Birmingham when we did.

My father's intention was to traverse the Blue Ridge Mountains in mid-afternoon and get to Bristol by nightfall. But in early afternoon just outside Albemarle we had a flat tire. We all got out to examine it. A person could put a fist in the hole. My father changed the tire, and we drove on to the next town to buy another one. No one bothered to comment much. A simple flat tire wasn't so bad considering what it might have been and in fact what we all believed it yet would be, a busted radiator or a gas tank that just fell off or exploded. We thought we were pretty lucky so far.

We stopped at a blue and white Pure Oil station. My father went to talk to the manager, and my mother went to the women's room. There was a lubrication rack in the back where we were parked, and beyond it was a storeroom, and inside the storeroom were cases and cases of ginger ale. We children had a little talk about that ginger ale. We weren't the spoiled darlings of the rich who could have a dozen soft drinks any time we asked. We didn't stop driving except for gas and meals, and even when we did stop there was no certainty we would be allowed a soft drink. My brother John and I decided this was a once-in-a-lifetime chance we couldn't afford to pass up, even if Mary and George wouldn't join us.

We snuck into the storeroom and brought back, two-by-two, a dozen small bottles of ginger ale. We hid them on the back floor under the overhang the seat made. Wordlessly, Ida watched us, and we said, "You can have some."

Fifty miles or so down the road the bottles came loose and began to roll around on the back floor. Desperately John and I tried to get them under control. I motioned to Ida to lean forward so I could stuff a couple behind the seat. She said, in a voice that overrode the wind sounds from open windows,

"John and Nancy stole a mighty lot of pop."

John and I were so stunned that we had not the presence of mind to deny it. Despite a long sad history of betrayal, we children always believed Ida was on our side. Time after time we confided secrets to her, which she, for reasons of her own, soon shared with Mother. Thus she initiated us in a way our parents never dared into the changingness, the convenience, the honest *quid pro quo* of love.

My father slammed on the brakes and angled for the shoulder. The face he turned to us contained a double message: We had dishonored him and we had destroyed his only holiday. "We'll have to go back to return them," he said.

John bit his lip. I began to whimper.

Mother said, "But that'll take a couple of hours. We'll be in the mountains when it turns dark."

My father said, "It can't be helped." He stuck his head out of the window to see if he could make his U-turn.

"Dear God, not the mountains at night," Mother said. She reached across George and touched my father's hand on the steering wheel. "God! I don't think I could stand it."

He pulled his head back in to look at her. They stared at each other for a moment. He sighed, shifted gears, then gained the roadway and went straight on, toward Bristol. I watched his eyes in the rearview mirror. Slowly they began to change and then he glanced at Mother and began to smile ruefully.

"Everybody's honor has a price," he said. "Nancy's and John's is a bottle of pop. Yours is not crossing the mountains at night."

"And yours?" Mother asked. We all knew he was eager to tell her.

"Mine? Mine is not listening to you nag poor old defenseless God an extra hundred miles." Everybody laughed.

I thoroughly misunderstood his shift of mood. "We'll open them tonight. We were going to share anyway."

He said, "For the rest of the trip, you will not have a single bottle of pop, nor will either of you get to sit by the window until we get to Birmingham."

Mother said, "Ida, please hand me the bottles."

Mother and Ida took turns tossing the bottles at trees and posts along the way, exclaiming gleefully when they hit something. My father must have thought it looked like fun.

"Let me try one," he said. Ida put a bottle in his hand. Mother cleared her throat. He tossed the bottle over the top of the car and then turned to watch its descent into the wirey brush. "Not a bad shot," he said. The car swerved.

"Lord help me," Mother said. She slammed on her set of the brakes.

"Better save your prayers," he said. "We're just getting to the scary part."

In the distance we could see the bluish spread of evergreens rising steeply to meet the afternoon sun. If we peered intently, we could see the little road like a pencil line, back and forth, all the way to the top.

"Look at that sight," my father said. "Look at that cloud formation. Look at those magnificent trees. Why, they're thick as cream in there."

"Dear God," Mother said. "Keep your eye on the road."

He laughed and talked and looked and gesticulated, and we were so distracted by his gaiety that before we were fully prepared for our ordeal, we were in the middle of it. That mountain road was more or less hand over hand, and the hairpin turns were so sharp that our running board scraped as we turned up. Between hairpins was a little more than a dozen carlengths, and sometimes off the low side it seemed the fall would be forever.

My mother said, "You're going too fast for these turns."

"Look at the fog. Now isn't that nice?" He stuck his head out the window. "By gum, that was a possum. Mary, take a look." He maneuvered another switchback.

Mary said, "I don't see anything."

"Right in the crotch of that big tree." The car was going in one direction, and he was looking in the other.

Mother reached for the steering wheel, catching George on the chin. My father came back into the car and pushed her hand away. "The last time you did that," he said in a conversational tone, "we sideswiped a truck."

She was a pushover. "If I hadn't, we'd have hit it head-on. Isn't that so, children?"

Witnesses last autumn outside Atlanta, we were jurors now. We took our duties seriously. We nodded, for her to see, but remained quiet, for him not to hear.

The car swerved again. "Was that an eagle or a hawk? Gosh, I'm glad we came this route. It's wonderful. Just look." His eyes scanned the darkening valley.

Mother decided on a different tack. "It is nice, but won't it get dark?"

"Happens every night," he replied.

Ida gave a shriek of laughter, then bit her fingers. He turned around to get from her face the full pleasure of his joke. The right rear wheel of the car slid off the pavement. He whipped the steering wheel around and the wheel sank in the muck of mountain lushness. The car came to rest on a slight incline of limestone that Mother's prayers must have got for us. We weren't far off the road, only a foot or two, but through the back window we saw nothing but sky. When my father got out of the car, it rocked ominously. The left rear wheel was not quite touching the ground. Dusk gathered. The fog lowered.

We believed that he would save us. He was our protector, our hero, the solid substance in our lives. This message came from Mother. And we feared that we would die. This message likewise came to us from Mother. He was going to kill us. I know she believed in him and trusted him, but I know too that a part of her, not an inconsequential part, hoped that he would fail. Written on her face become as narrow as a knife blade, her tightened eyes, her pinched nose, the tensely immobilized shoulders was her desire for his failure, to pay him back for her panic and anxiety of the moment and the nameless pains of their life together.

"All right," he said. "I see what to do. Stay put, everybody."

"We will do no such thing," my mother said. At a signal from her, we fled the car and stood in the roadway. Our father chuckled, to show the tolerant amusement of God at the trivial agnosticism of man. Duke raced back and forth, snuffling under rotten logs, looking for quarry.

My father set to work. Though he was a man whose life work had been purely the use of this intelligence, he was countrybred and like most country boys believed that he could do any chore. His belief was unrelated to reality. When he replaced a windowpane, he broke the sash. When he spliced a wire, he blew a fuse. He went through life postponing the time and increasing the need for the plumber, the electrician, the mechanic.

The quality he was proudest of was his ingenuity. Any time he found a round-about, unexpected way to solve a problem, he was delighted with himself. Never mind that the ingenuity led to failure, even disaster. I have that trait myself and it is like drink or drugs. Addicts will suspend a crystal chandelier from pipe cleaners and paper clips or fasten a broken sofa leg with chewing gum and thread. Eventually, of course, the chandelier falls, the sofa collapses, taking a table and vase with it, but we learn nothing. We can't resist the temptation, we can't remember the hangover.

After his quick survey of the situation, my father hoisted an immense rock onto his thighs and dropped it near the free-spinning wheel. He found several large logs, six or eight inches thick and only beginning to rot a bit, and with them he constructed a pyramid woodpile behind each back wheel. He bent several saplings until they snapped, sharpened their points with his pocketknife and jammed them into the damp earth behind the pyramids. He sharpened two tall saplings and stuck them in the ground alongside the wheels, angled out so that they touched the back bumper and their free ends were in the air. He wiped his hands on pine needles and smiled benignly at this handiwork.

All this had taken about ten minutes. On the roadway the rest of us watched silently. Mother kept shaking her head, unbelieving and scornful. She was as naturally handy as my father always believed he was.

"Now I need a little help," my father said. "George and John, come help. Time you learned how to do things." He directed their attention to his construction. "The woodpile will keep the car from sliding back." He pulled back on one of the saplings stuck in by the wheels. "This works on the principle of the lever. Having the poles long increases your power so you can hoist the car. I'll fire it up and when I yell, then you hoist. Do you understand?"

"Pretty knobby," said John admiringly. He too was an addict of ingenuity.

George was not. "Suppose the car slips backwards?"

My father regarded him for a long moment. "Jump, then," he said in a tone that made George wince.

Mother came down off the road. "All that's totally unnecessary," she said. "But if you insist on doing it, Ida and I will help. You boys move aside."

Ida was as proud as Jephthah's daughter, ready to be sacrificed. She asked no quarter, she did not volunteer, she waited.

My father waved Mother off. "No, no," he said, "if you women got hurt, I'd never hear the end of it." He winked at Ida.

Mother walked right into the trap. "And what about the boys? Suppose they get hurt because of your ridiculous. . . ."

He said, "Are you suggesting that I don't care about the welfare of my sons?" Speechless with fake outrage, he stared at her as if she were a common criminal. All their years together he did that to her, kept her off balance by employing a slippery conglomeration of sophistry, righteousness, and *non sequitur*. Finally she too learned the technique and became a formidable player of the game, moving with lightning speed from untenable position to untenable position.

Before she could figure out an answer, he had gotten in the car, gunned the motor, and yelled "Hoist" to the boys. By the time George and John had grappled their way to the top of the poles, the car was on the road. It bucked, coughed, died, but it did not slip back. Though everyone knew they hadn't done a thing, the boys raised a proud cheer and made for the front seat as their reward. Mother usually sat in front because she believed she drove better there, but in the midst of victory and defeat she resigned herself to the rear. We were soon off again, catastrophe surmounted once more.

As we straightened up after the next hairpin, my father shot Mother a look in the rearview mirror, and said, "Well, aren't you going to say anything?"

All of us tensed up, waiting for the confrontation between them— the real catastrophe we all feared. We were still on the mountain, still ascending to the pass, and we had several hours of driving before Bristol.

Would she give into her anger and blame him, tell him how reckless he had been, how it had been all his fault, and how incompetent, how useless had been his clever ingenuity? She had the power to ruin the trip for him, to bring him down off his peak of lightheartedness and face the reality of our danger. Would she express her own anxiety or would she soothe his? All these thoughts swept through us in waves of emotion, not so neatly formulated then as now but more powerful for being inchoate, unspeakable. We waited.

She tossed her head like a flirtatious girl pretending anger. She said, "You get us into these fixes just so you can get us out and be a hero."

We all laughed, far beyond the merit of her humor. Especially my father laughed, a gay and grateful laugh. Then he said in his teasing voice, "Look at that little pocket of light down there in the valley. Look at that bird silhouetted against the sky. Look. . . ."

"Lord help us," Mother said. "Look out. Dear God."

Lee's Lieutenants

IN THE LATE 1930s, my family moved back to Birmingham to live. Although we children had only spent two summer months in Alabama, while my father politicked, we considered it home. We were going home, home to the South.

I was twelve and entered the eighth grade of the neighborhood school. My parents were not the kind to pave the way for us by identifying themselves to the school authorities or calling on old acquaintances whose children might be our classmates. We were on our own. I did not know one child. On the first day the teacher invited me to say my name and where I was from. When I said, "Washington," the class let out a hoot of derision, and I felt my face flame.

That night I asked my mother what was so funny about coming from Washington, and she said, "Don't say Warshington. It doesn't have an 'r' in it."

That these Southern children found me so odd and unacceptable injured me. I wanted desperately to belong with them. Although by nature more outspoken than timid, more bellicose than silent in suffering, I felt then as if I were nothing but tiny white fragile bones and pale freckles. I sat in class for weeks without speaking, practicing silently the wide open trusting innocent sound of the Southern vowel.

Our history lessons during that first term had to do with the War Between the States—Southerners did not call it the Civil War. During those first silent friendless weeks, I spent hours in the library, reading avidly about great ante-bellum plantations with thousands of slaves, limitless acres of rich black soil, and the cotton lushly spreading westward. Sitting with the book open before me, I dreamed that my great-grandfather had personified that rich, that gloriously old South. As I watched dustmotes swimming in the sunlight, I borrowed great luxury and power from his imagined past, and I wore them as my present own.

But even as I floated down the curving solid mahogany staircase, my gloved hand trailing greetings over the shiny banister, glistening eyes taking in the loving admiration of my classmates waiting in the throng below, my daydream was cut short by the imagined appearance of my father. First he was in the crowd, and then he was the crowd. His frown told me that my posturing pretense betrayed all that he valued in our real past. And so, shamed, I grasped the book tighter and drove my eyes down the pages to find someone else's manifest destiny.

My father was deeply proud of being a Huddleston and a Southerner, but it was an honest pride tempered by history. He had been born in 1869 in middle Tennessee on the Murphreesboro Pike that Sherman had marched down on his way to Georgia. My recollection of that part of Tennessee is of gigantic boulders of limestone jutting out of limey soil, of a pervading flatness and scrub pine and a low wirey bush so pungent you could taste it as you walked by. That land was not fit for the cotton economy, but my father said that before the Civil War his grandfather had a fairly large farm worked by ten or twelve hands.

After the War, most of the land was sold for taxes and my great-grandfather was hard put to feed his family. He got mighty little help from his many sons, my father said, for they were so ashamed of working the fields that whenever a carriage or horse passed by they ducked below the level of the corn to protect their honor from the view of ex-slaves and scalawags and social inferiors.

"Protect their honor?" my father repeated, outraged, gazing around the dinner table at each of us as if we had called it honor. "Bosh. Honor would have set to work and amounted to something and got the land back." That generation, he said, had not been trained to work, and the sons had been demoralized by the War.

He said it was the next generation—his sturdy yeoman cousins who had stayed on in Tennessee—who through frugality and hard labor had earned back the lost land, the lost pride. The price they had paid was a life of meagerness and isolation. Of ten children in one family, four had never married, two had married cousins, two had married when they were nearly fifty (as had my father), and only three of the ten had children. They were without self-pity and they were cold. Once my father complained about an undue show of emotion in our family and sternly reprimanded us children with, "Huddlestons don't gush," but quick as a wink my mother shot back, "And Huddlestons don't marry either; they mostly just dry up and blow away." Thus was ambivalence nurtured in our family.

Opinion on secession had sharply divided Tennessee, and the state sent half as many men to the Union Army as to the Confederate. So far as we know, our family was all on the Confederate side. One uncle of my father's died at Antietam, and another had a leg amputated in a Yankee prison camp.

My grandfather did not serve in the Confederate Army although he was old enough to be a soldier. I believe this fact rankled in my father and shamed him. He would never have spoken this shame, for filial loyalty was a high value to him, but it showed in the careful way he told us his father had not served, and it showed in the admiration he expressed for the Uncle George he had never seen, killed, and Uncle Billy, one-legged for the Lost Cause.

And I think it may have been this shame that curbed in him the Southern fault of family glorification. What he honored was not the romance of family riches or accomplishment or derring-do, but the simple country fact of kinship. He wrote a book entitled *Huddleston Family Tables* which used courthouse records to trace the lineage of the Huddlestons in the United States. It is a book of begats, not of celebration. Once a supposedly educated man named Huddleston sent my father a family tree prepared by a commercial firm. The line went something like Cedric, Nordic, Athelstan, Huddleston. My father wrote him, "If you believe this you should immediately lay claim to the British throne."

Anyone who bore our name was a welcome guest in our house. During World War II when I was sixteen, I saw a friend off at the train station and, glancing idly at a suitcase tag nearby, I saw that it belonged to a Lt. Huddleston. I went up to the man standing alongside it and said, "Are you Lt. Huddleston?" and pointed at the tag. He said, "Go away, I'm not interested." But I persisted until he recognized what an innocent I was. He was from Kansas, stationed in Alabama, and he said he would call us on his next leave.

When I told this story at home, my older sisters were mortified, but my father said, "Nanny did the proper thing. He's a Huddleston after all." The lieutenant did call and over the next six months visited us several times, although we girls and our friends found him boring if rather good-looking.

But they did not have to be lieutenants and good-looking, they just had to be Huddlestons. At noon one Sunday, a man and a woman appeared at our door. They said they were Huddlestons from the Northwest, just passing through, and they wanted to pay respects to my father. It was clear to us children that the man was a drunken derelict come for a handout and the woman was a moron and perhaps a prostitute with a black satin dress and spike heels. They sat with my father in our living room and with his help soon found their table in the genealogy book. My father took my mother aside and asked, "What are we having for Sunday dinner?" My mother threw her hands up and answered, "One thing we are not having is them." He said, "That man's a Huddleston. They can't all be rich and beautiful." And my mother said, "And they can't all sit at my table, either." He shot her a gloomy look, but he knew he wasn't going to win on that one. The best he could do was to keep them talking for another half hour or so until the dinner was cold.

My father never took a vacation, never went to New York, never sat on a beach. When he was given tickets to army horse shows or the Alabama-GWU football games or for a box at the President's Inaugural Parade, he gave them to friends and neighbors. But occasionally on a Sunday he gathered his resigned wife and his recalcitrant children and drove off to a battlefield of the Civil War. We paid calls at all the battlefields within a hundred mile radius of Washington, Birmingham, or Murfreesboro, Tennessee. We children

31

were thus initiated into the mystery beyond blood kin: the South, the Lost Cause.

In my memories of these trips, I see undulating hillocks and green valleys and in the distance the black-green trees shielding the darkness beyond. And of course the silver observation tower. These towers, I believe constructed by the WPA, perch on skinny rickety legs and the platform above sways and vibrates in the wind. Nonetheless my father, intensely excited by the adventure, charges up the narrow silver steps, drawing us after him.

I see myself as last in line. With each step up my anxiety increases. I cast a hopeful complaining glance down to my lucky mother who sits safely on the ground, leaning against the picnic hamper, shading her eyes as she watches over our ascent.

"Hurry, Nanny," my father shouts down to me in an unusually light voice. "I see old Sheridan coming out of the woods already."

My legs ache. My hair twists in the wind and blinds me. I am the youngest, the baby, least expected to cooperate, most forgivable. "Mother," I call in a frightened voice. I see her swing to her knees, ready to spring, her hand held in the air to keep me from falling. I decide I will go to her, and I start down.

"Nancy doesn't give a hoot for Marse Robert or any of them." It is the voice of my brother, and without faltering I ascend the ladder.

From these towers we could see miles in all directions. At the start of the lecture, my father pointed us toward the Confederate lines. ("Uncle George was here, wasn't he, Daddy?" "No, he was not at this battle." "But Uncle George was a major, wasn't he, or was he a colonel?" "He was a private, and a brave one.") My father knew it all by heart, could and did tell us the generals and colonels on both sides, the number of foot soldiers, horse, cannon. As we listened and watched, he created armies for us out of the high grass, and we could hear the sound of battle in the creaking of the tower and the wind.

None of us was more excited than my father was himself. As the opposing armies drew together, he crept to the guardrail and leaned far out, as if to see around a stand of trees to the hidden cavalry ready to come up. Then came my mother's voice: "Hold him, children, don't let him fall."

He gazed down at her and began to laugh, all the while dipping out over the rail dangerously, pointing, gesturing, declaiming on the virtues of Southern generals. And so we observed one more episode of the teasing play between them, that safety valve of emotion that allowed my father to believe that Huddlestons don't gush.

My memory still holds the spot where my father reckoned the South lost the War, that spot where Stonewall Jackson was accidentally killed by his own men—irony of awfullest irony, for, my father said, Jackson was the only man Lee could truly depend on. And I remember the woods outside Frederick where D.H. Hill lost his orders, his three cigars, and his honor. And the place near Verdiersville where the irrepressible Jeb Stuart left his plumed hat.

We climbed the tower at Gettysburg, and for an hour or so that three-day battle unfolded before us. First came Stuart, sent to reconnoiter but blithely driving so far east that he arrived exhausted and useless. Here was brave, cautious Dick Ewell with his wooden leg splintered by a cannonball. And there was Longstreet, that great tactician, stubborn and too proud. And Union General Meade on the high ground of Cemetery Ridge, given so much time that his reinforcements came and he was more than ready to fight. Finally, there came Pickett and his men, too late, too few, but doggedly charging for the glory of Virginia, until the field was laden with the dead and injured heroes.

Ten years or so later in college, I wrote a paper analyzing the Battle of Gettysburg. I knew what I thought of Longstreet's willfulness, Stuart's bravado, Pickett's foolish courage. But it was only after an emotional struggle that I could hold Lee responsible for the defeat. Blaming Lee was simply not in my father's lexicon of criticism. For so many of his generation, Lee embodied only and all that was good in the South, honor, kindliness, social sensitivity, reserve, and the glad sacrifice of self to Cause. If for Northerners, it is Lincoln's humanity that touches the deepest emotions, for Southerners it is Lee's sublimity, perhaps because the need for transcendence was so great, the pride so injured.

When we came down the tower steps, we were transformed. We were not afraid of the wind or the trembling tower, or even of our father. We had undergone a catechism and been anointed Confederates of the Lost Cause. We felt close to that formidable man we lived with, we were of his family, of his place, we marched to the same drummer, and we were as tender and sorrowful as he was. All the way home, we sang songs, the sad songs first, and then the ones like "Old Joe Hooker, come out the Wilderness, come out the Wilderness," and our father sang with us.

For weeks after each outing, my brothers and I played Civil War. No one in our Washington neighborhood knew much about the War, and we might have got away with any variation. But sticking to the truth was an expression of camaraderie with our father and a show of pride at being Southern, no matter the defeat.

In our games, my brothers were always the leaders of opposing sides. But for re-enacting the Civil War, they were both Confederates. One brother would be Robert E. Lee, and the other would be Stonewall Jackson. Being the youngest and only girl allowed to play, I had no real status in the neighborhood gang, but for this game I had a choice role: Jeb Stuart because I was a Huddleston and an authentic Southerner.

The other kids were given roles in accordance with their friendship with my brothers. Out of favor, one boy might be Longstreet, for his meanness, or Bragg, for his name, and a special favorite might be Pelham or Early. The neighborhood sissy was included in the game, and he was called U.S. Grant and sent to stand at the steps that led to the janitor's room at the church on the corner.

And then with a shrill rebel yell ringing down the Shenandoah, across Chickamauga, past Chancellorsville, we charged forth. We circled the block, scaled fences, smashed flowers, and, shrieking, swooped down on the hapless Grant. The enemy was ours. Never before had Confederates such numerical superiority. Grant's armies were pinned, his glasses removed, his hair rumpled, and then guiltily Lee would say, "Ah, nuts, it's time for Appomattox." He would surrender his sword so vigorously that Grant would burst into tears.

We children were glad when the family moved back to Alabama. Though most of us had been born in Washington, and all of us had lived our lives there, had gone to school there, had our friends there, we were never of that cold foreign city. We always knew we were Southerners. We expected to find in Birmingham an overwhelming commonality we had not known in exile.

The South in those days was not a transient society, and the children in my class had been together since kindergarten. They were old friends, and I was a stranger. But I interpreted their exclusivity as a misunderstanding of who I was and what I stood for. In the early days, the teacher had tried to help me with my isolation by finding me some prestige. Once she asked me if I had ever been to Harper's Ferry. I gladly said yes, thinking that my wide travels and sophistication would bring me some credit. But it was, I had to conclude, a mistake. Looking around the room at the blank, unsmiling faces, I thought the kids believed I was a carpetbagger, come out of the far north city of Washington to pillage and to burn. I did not know how to tell them what a Confederate I was, how I had fought alongside my father at Bull Run and Antietam and Chattanooga.

And then the opportunity came. When we finished studying the Civil War, the teacher asked the class, "How many of you wish the South had won the War?"

My hand shot skyward, and I turned around in my chair to claim my fellow rebels. No other hand was raised. Thirty-two Southern kids sat stonily at their desks. Burning with embarrassment, I lowered my arm. But then I thought, Was no one loyal in defeat? Would no one uphold Lee, Jackson? I raised my arm again, still alone.

That night after dinner, I said to my father, "I'm the only real Southerner in that dumb class."

He asked me how I had come to that conclusion, and I told him about the teacher's question. I'm sure my voice had a bragging edge to it.

He said, "Oh, they're Southerners all right. They meant they were against slavery is all. If you wish the South had won, that must mean you approve of one human being able to own another."

"I don't care about all that," I said. "I just wish the South had won, and if that means slavery, well then. . ."

"Don't talk like an ass," he said. "Slavery is a terrible evil. It degrades both sides."

After a suitable pause, I said, "Well, but the Confederates must have believed it was all right."

"I'm sorry to say that at that time, most Southerners did think it was all right. And the South paid for it."

I loved to catch him. Slyly I said, "I thought you would have been a Confederate."

He sighed. "No doubt I would have been with my people, right or wrong, foolish or wise."

"Robert E. Lee believed in slavery," I said.

"There's where you're dead wrong," he answered in a proud voice. "Not Marse Robert. He freed his slaves before the War. But he loved his people and so he fought with them. Anyway, Nanny, you mustn't judge one time in history by the conscience of another. Lee did what he thought was honorable and right for him at that time. I hope you do as well. It isn't all that simple and easy."

I was stung by that. It did seem simple and easy, yet it was complicated, too. I had not focused on slavery before. At school the next morning I said—in my old Yankee voice, for I did not want to care whether they misunderstood my motives or not—"I'm glad the North won the War. The Confederates were wrong."

No one seemed to care, one way or the other. Soon enough time and custom healed the wound of my loneliness and I sufficiently belonged. And as our biographies have turned out, I have been more open and eager for social change than the others in that class, by our common lights. But just then, inside, a large part of me was crying for our people, for the Lost Cause, for the fallen Jackson and the rollicking Stuart, for Lee, and I would be forever escaping the ambivalence toward love and conscience that trapped me then.

The Man Who Hated Cigarettes

My father's views on smoking were as significant to us as another man's views on God or Hitler might have been to his children. He was as aware of religion as the next man and no doubt more concerned with Hitler than most. But it was smoking that really got him.

I remember once—some time in the early 1930s when I was seven and he was in his sixties—he came home laughing to himself, wiping the grin off his mouth. Our mother always toadied to his rare gay moods, and she called together an audience of us children to hear his story.

At lunch in a crowded, cramped restaurant, he had dug his spoon into a grapefruit and a drop shot off on to the neck of a woman at the next table. Just thinking of it, he laughed so that his shoulders bounced and his face collapsed. He had twisted the grapefruit around to go after another section, and this time he hit the woman in the ear. When she turned, he hid the grapefruit behind cupped hands and played innocent. Then he decided he would try to control his shot, and just as the stream left the fruit the woman turned again and caught the juice right above the eye.

He had been stuttering and gasping, but he sobered to say, "Of course I would never have tried such a thing, but she was smoking." *Smoking.* He spat out the word as if the flavor disgusted him. Womanizers, drunkards, petty thieves and swindlers—toward them he had pity, even tolerance, perhaps understanding. But tobacco smokers were beyond belief. They were just plain bad.

Yet even here, where private disgusts and taboos coalesced so powerfully, he had devised a subtle hierarchy of badness. Snuff dipping was not unknown in the backwoods of our Southern family. It was not widespread and never indulged publicly, but to my father it was the most acceptable way to use tobacco. Perhaps this was the defiant country boy in him, the successful Public Man who would not betray his plain origins. The snuff dippers were old women who had borne the brunt of Reconstruction more nobly than the startled and refined men in the family, and perhaps my father thought they bore it with the help from the chewed matchstick dipped in the snuff can.

Next down from the women who dipped were men who chewed. A filthy thing by our standards, but country and manly, and, as my father said, anybody who could hold the stuff in his mouth, stand the harsh flavor, and endure the slime sliding down his throat was paid off and proved out. Once we visited a cousin who operated a store on a dirt road off the Murphreesboro Pike in Tennessee. Sitting on a keg of nails while my father joshed the men, I thought I spied the remains of a Moon Pie in the corner of a box, and I wet my finger and went for it. Ever since tasting those crumbs of plug tobacco, I have had the highest respect for anyone who chewed.

Pipe smoking was dangerous to life and limb, but my father thought it was abidable if a man indulged only while walking outside after meals. It had no special plus in his mind, for it was not country or Southern, but he thought it was self-limiting for being so much trouble.

In those days, cigars were rare. Movie gangsters could be identified by them, and so could sharpies on the street. My father claimed that he had smoked one when he was twenty and thus knew whereof he spoke: cigar smoking was sickening and self-indulgent and showed a weakness of character.

He saved his real scorn for cigarettes, however. Old men who

smoked cigarettes were fools, young men were knaves, and women . . .
if women who smoked cigarettes were not moral degenerates, of easy
virtue and ill repute, they ought to quit the advertising.

And so of course his wife and all of his five children ended up
smoking cigarettes. So did their spouses, their friends, the young
women whose company he admired in his last years, the young men
he enjoyed and envied. It was like a conspiracy to offend him. And yet
no one who cared about him at all, or even in any serious way
acknowledged his presence, ever lit up in front of him. I mean that: no
one.

It is part of the family lore that my mother started smoking on a
dare issued by my father's favorite aunt. This aunt was not a
backwoods woman but a sophisticated and well-traveled lady. Her side
of my father's family had been less well off before the Civil War and
so gave up its ante-bellum ways earlier and got to the city sooner. She
took my mother under her wing and taught her how to smoke.

My mother was twenty-two years younger than my father, and it
required ingenuity and exercise to stay fit for the years' long struggle.
Having chanced—if it was not carefully calculated—upon cigarettes as
the ground for skirmishing, she may have saved them from war. She
was red-headed, feisty, tough, and she smoked, but he was what he
was, and she did not smoke in front of him. Not even on the forty-five-
minute ride to the emergency room of the hospital to see my brother,
who had been seriously hurt in a wreck. After a heart attack, my
mother gave up smoking, and I believe it took several months for their
relationship to recover.

We children began to smoke all at about the same time. We were
very close in age, maintained a hot competition down the line, and
passed along vices and privileges as quickly as we found them.

The eldest, Mary, went off to college just before her sixteenth
birthday. She was slender, pretty, shy, much oppressed as the eldest by
our watchful father, much burdened by a passel of younger children.
She was an undeveloped country ripe for freedom's excesses.

That summer when the family went to Birmingham, my father
stayed on in Washington to debate the Guffey Coal Bill. We had not
seen Mary since Christmas, and we wondered what she had become.
On the second day we younger children peered over the transom above

her locked door and saw her blowing smoke out the window into the sycamore tree. This find was first-quality serendipity: we only spied to annoy. We said share or else, and share she did.

We soon learned that smoking was an expensive proposition. We pooled our resources and found them wanting. We scoured alleys for Coke and Nehi bottles to reclaim the deposits. Regularly the man who bought old gold came around and one by one we lost last year's Christmas watch to two packs of Chesterfields. Finally we laid siege to the local drugstore. While the druggist coped at the back of the store—where some of us fingered the magazines and drew perilously close to Evening in Paris perfume—one of us crept off with a flat fifty tin of cigarettes.

Unused to middle-class delinquency, the druggist could not believe what instinct told him about us. He often asked our names and we said, "Buzzie and Sistie and Fala and we hate war." We said, daring to come close, "John and Nancy Garner." "Pecksniff," said my brother, and I said, "Ralph Henry Barbour." We were summertime marauders without a care in the world, and our timing was superb: he never caught us in the act.

When the Guffey Coal Bill passed, so did our vices. Our father's nose was too acute for us to dare to smoke and the thought of his learning we had stolen was too awful to bear. But we all vowed to grow up to be true smokers, if not thieves.

When we moved to Birmingham permanently in 1937, I was twelve, weighed no more than eighty pounds, had straight red hair and a million freckles, and was devoid of breasts and hips. Mine was not merely the face of a child but of a particularly innocent one. When my brother would say, "I've seen high brows and I've seen low brows, but, kid, you're my first no brows," I was grateful for the attention.

Yet it set me thinking, and I thought that with a Chesterfield between my lips, I'd be a knockout. I began to buy cigarettes. I thought I looked twenty-three in a breeze. In the downtown lunch counter where my friends and I ate chicken salad after the Saturday Mickey Mouse Club, older people watched me smoke and whispered: Who is that fascinating young woman? The boys in my eighth grade class, and high school boys, too, stared at me and giggled with desire and longing. They kept their distance because obviously I was too old for them.

Fairly soon I saw how exhausting it was to be a *femme fatale*, and I fell back, cigarettes in hand, upon a role that suited me better: comedienne, performer. As a juggler had tenpins and Frank Buck his lions and his chair, I had my cigarettes. I became an *artiste* of smoking. My technique evolved over the next four years. Whenever the crowd looked elsewhere, I tried a new trick. While my friends were still coughing when they inhaled, I started blowing smoke through my nose. When they caught up, I went for the smoke ring: two, ten, twenty, fifty on a single puff. I blew a kind of ring through my nose, two at a time, five times a puff. As I wiggled my ears, I put cigarettes into my nose, inhaled, and blew smoke rings out of my mouth. I concealed a lighted cigarette in my mouth. I learned that the thick coating of the tongue was an ashtray into which one might stub out a cigarette. At last, after much wearying practice, I broke the local—perhaps the international—record for smoke rings on one puff. I blew one hundred and eighteen.

As I sat there in my sister Jane's room, nausea flowed through me. But crowds cheered, friends laughed, even brothers and sisters applauded enviously. The door opened, and there stood my father.

"Someone," he said, "is smoking."

I gazed around. All the others had doused their cigarettes. Was it a gang-up? Was this their gratitude? But I did not waste time on theory: I stomped out my cigarette on the hardwood floor. If, I thought, you keep swallowing, the smoke disappears through the gut. I swallowed and swallowed. Smoke hung several feet thick in the room.

My father backed off from the poisonous fumes. "Who is smoking?"

What shall I say we said? This kind of episode was repeated so often that I hesitate to favor one particular lie. "Mother just left the room," we often said, relying on her known guilt. Or we pointed to a distant relative we did not much fancy, to a sometime friend, to a single-shot sojourner in our midst. "What the hell, why blame me?" the victim might later say. And we answered, "Because it won't matter for you." That, if I ever heard one, was a self-fulfilling prophecy. That person was no longer welcome in our house.

Sometimes when my father asked, "Who is smoking?" we answered, "No one is smoking." We did not trouble to differentiate "is" from "was." Did that make us liars, cheats, dishonorable children of an honorable father? Clearly not. Was it our fault if after half a century of law and politics he did not know how to elicit information?

After we would give our shyster answers, he would gaze around at the smoke, smile mildly, draw his brows together, shake his head. To indicate what? That he believed us? Did not believe us? Did not wish to make an issue but yet to make the point? That his sense of betrayal was too profound for words? He departed and in his wake were half a dozen clever, triumphant, joyous, relieved, guilty, somehow gratified, somehow very pained teen-agers mouthing their next weed.

Like apostles the world over, we spread the gospel. We initiated all our friends into the joys of tobacco and the fear of our father. Though he almost never raised his voice and was quiet and scholarly for a politician, everyone saw in him the wrath of Moses, the judgment of Noah, the rectitude of Washington. The most brazen hid to smoke. When I was fourteen, I made friends with a bunch of girls considerably older than I, freshmen in college, roustabouts, mischief-makers enjoying a late but lively adolescence. I was a wildly applauding audience to their reckless driving of one family's old Terraplane, to sprinkling frogs in the beds of their dormmates, to secreting the rubber rattlesnake in the closet of the dorm mother. And I had my own act: smoking. Oddly, they had never smoked until I came along and they had no special talent for it. In most adventures, I was mascot. In smoking I was champ.

For reasons no longer clear in memory, one of the girls was suspended from the university. One Friday at dusk they tooted a strange horn in front of my house, a U-Drive-It horn. "Get a toothbrush, get your money, invent a story, and let's go," one of them said when I trotted out.

It wasn't all that easy, but then it wasn't all that hard, either. As I walked to the front door, I concocted a story: dinner and a movie, a slumber party, and tomorrow morning a trip to Tuscaloosa—with my friend's mother, of course. After rearing so many children, my parents were exhausted and had come to trust less in control and more in the natural good judgment of good blood. But they had misgivings.

"Wellll," my mother began.

"Thanks, old top," I said, patting her on the head, and I sped out the door.

By hook or crook, we got hold of a case of beer, bought some potato chips and cigarettes, and set out in that rented car to all four points of the compass, looking to raise hell at every college in the state of Alabama. We climbed fire escapes at Birmingham-Southern, threw pebbles at a fraternity house window in Tuscaloosa where my friends had beaux, roared through the Montevallo campus sitting on the horn at 3 a.m. and sped on, laughing, drinking, tossing lighted cigarettes into the vanishing night. At five o'clock we parked on a lonely stretch of highway in northern Alabama and the other four slept while I kept watch. I was prouder than I was afraid.

We stopped once more before we got back to Birmingham, at a tourist court on the Bessemer Highway where we ate cheese crackers with peanut butter and drank coffee, and all of us slept for three hours. When we woke up we took cold showers and then we headed home in earnest.

To avoid detection—we all had different lies—I was deposited at a drugstore while the others reported home. Drained of everything, including restlessness, I waited patiently for them to return. When I saw my brother drive by, I waved, and he made a U-turn and came back.

"I've got a ride," I said in a cool voice.

He said, "Forget it, the jig's up, get in."

And so the jig was up, had been for eighteen hours, when my mother's intuition (or memory of her own adolescence or understanding of mine) had prompted her to drive to my friend's house, ostensibly to bring me money for that dinner, that movie.

My brother told me that the highway patrol was on the lookout, but no one knew about the U-Drive-It. The dean of women had been alerted, but not the fraternity boys, not the girls whose sleep we jubilantly fractured. I see that six-block ride home all in red, painted so by my exhaustion and fear, by my silent vow to be tough, by a sudden understanding of the night my parents had spent on a roller coaster of fright and fury.

My father was sitting on the sofa, playing solitaire. I said, "I know I've done wrong and caused you a lot of worry, and I'm ready for any punishment you give me." I meant it, too. There was my prime victim, my mother, standing in the kitchen door, chalk-white, with trembling lips and little-eyed from crying.

My father said, "We all make mistakes, Nanny."

If he had struck me or railed at me or even refused to speak to me, I might have endured. But thus to speak, to think first of me, my need, to forgive so gently, exacting nothing—that undid me and I began to cry with great racks and sobbings. I was put to bed tenderly by my mother and slept all afternoon and all night and late into the next morning. But, waking, I was determined not to get off so easily, and I went in to my father.

"I want to tell you about it," I said.

"No need. We'll just forget it."

But I insisted and I told him. I told him about the U-Drive-It, the racing from campus to campus disturbing the world, about sleeping on the highway and then at the unsavory tourist court. And I told him we had bought a case of beer and drunk it.

He said, "I see it didn't kill you." He thought a moment, and then he said, "I suppose those older girls smoke."

"Yes."

It occurred to me how absurd his interest in that was, and yet how I had not mentioned that, pretending it was the least of it, knowing it was my real vulnerability with him.

He said, "I'd rather see you with the beer than with a cigarette, Nanny." He shuffled his chipped worn-out Bicycle cards and went on. "I believe I'll ask you—not *make*—ask you to stop being friends with those girls."

I said I would. It was little enough, and besides the whole thing had been a bit too rich for my blood. I didn't have to go to such extremes to make my rebellion, for I already smoked and that was rebellion enough. Never again did I go off on such a jaunt or cause my parents any worries outside the normal run. But I went on smoking.

About the time I turned sixteen, my mother conceded that since she was not able to stop her children's smoking—she had tried—she might as well join us. Her room became the favorite and safest place to congregate. After each meal all of us retired there to have our smoke. The bottom of her trash can was a layer of ash. Shake the curtains and blue-gray air bounced. The floor was pockmarked with hurriedly doused cigarettes when we heard our father's slippers slapping against his heels as he approached the room.

He usually sat alone in the living room playing solitaire, reading the paper, perhaps pondering the disappearance of his family. Often one of us might say, "Somebody ought to sit with Pappy," which had become our pet name for him during his old age. And one of us would, until our habit would call us away. In the summer we clustered on the front porch, and from the sofa it must have seemed to him the night was alight with fireflies—until he joined us. Sometimes he would come to bid us good night and perhaps join in the talk, until one by one we vanished, to smoke. For his very presence created awareness of a cigarette, and then a desire, and finally an overwhelming need. Although he was good company, full of old-time stories and quotations from Shakespeare, the Bible, the poets, full of hard-headed opinions about the world and history and money, our times with him grew less and less frequent for shorter and shorter intervals.

When we were older and came home to visit, he often sniffed a little and quite out of the blue asked one of us, "Do you smoke, Jane? Do you smoke, Nancy?"

By then I was a divided woman, divided between my desire to keep him from knowing I smoked and my yearning to be face to face with him. And I would answer, "Not all the time, Pappy."

"No one," he once responded, "smokes all the time. A body needs sleep." But that was the end of the probing—I don't think he really wanted to know.

He saw me only one time with a cigarette between my lips. And that was my wedding day. The ceremony took place at our house, and as the guests gathered below, my dearest friend and I were in my room. I was intensely nervous and faked whatever nervousness I did not come by honestly. I smoked feverishly as I donned my wedding clothes and fixed my face and hair and laughed uproariously over the absurdity of marriage, over the unredeemable absurdity of any marriage to which I was a party. I looked in the mirror, watching myself light another cigarette, turned to make another rueful joke, and faced my father.

He had come to fetch me. He had not seen me that morning and

45

had never seen my wedding gown. He stared at me a long moment and then said, "Smoking *cigarettes.*"

It brought me flat to earth and cleared my nerves. He was in his eighties then, and his eyes were faded and his awareness was not constant or sure. But at that moment (my wedding day!) he was deeply himself, and what he saw was not the finery but the cigarette, not the last departing daughter but the smoking child.

I said, "I thought it might calm my nerves." I pointed at my friend. "She gave it to me."

Below stairs, wedding music sounded. After a reproachful look, my friend began the procession. My father and I followed.

He died in his ninety-first year. Within six months two of his children, including me, had stopped smoking. Fear of cancer, we said, of heart attacks and asthma. Over the years, the two of us have discussed our quitting in a quiet, regretful, middle-aged way. We wonder if our father's dying made death real at last and made us more vulnerable to dying, now that he was dead. And we wonder if the need to smoke, to wage that one large battle against him, had died with him. And though neither of us believes in immortality, we ask each other if we had stopped smoking to please him and make ourselves proud of ourselves at last in our memory of him.

Yet when I am most strongly with that memory, I reproach myself and him. Perhaps there is always a false barrier between the generations, as absurd as smoking, but nonetheless I regret all of him I did not get to know and understand because I smoked and he would not tolerate it. And I wonder how we could have created such a thing.

46

Conversion and After

My FATHER'S FAVORITE JOKE symbolized our family's attitude toward religion. A little boy tattled to his Sunday School teacher that another little boy had said there wasn't a God. When the shocked teacher said, "And what did *you* say?" the little boy replied, "I said I don't care."

Neither of my parents ever went to church except on out-and-out political occasions. My mother always claimed she believed the usual, but she never did a thing to prove that she did. My father was an avowed disbeliever, but in the interests of a stable society he kept his scoffing within the family. His only indulgence was to tell his joke to his God-fearing country cousins and to devout preachers.

Yet every Sunday morning between September and June, which was the nine months we lived in Washington, our father sent all five of us children off to Sunday School. When we said he didn't set much of an example, he had a dozen replies. He said he had served his time. He said he had to tolerate a mighty lot of fools six days a week in the House of Representatives and even God rested on the seventh. He said we had a duty to find out what it was we weren't going to believe. Hiding a grin, he said, "All decent middle-class folks believe in God and go to church, so let's have no more fussing."

And so we went to whatever church was handiest, Methodist, Baptist, Presbyterian, and always we went reluctantly. We hated to relinquish our nickels to their collection plates, and half the time we lost them in the linings of our coats and searched frantically as the plate passed us. Often we did not make it to the church on time, or at all, for we stopped off at the local drugstore for a Coke and a half-hour of *Esquire*. The parents of our friends sometimes asked where we worshipped, and after I was eleven I always said Woods Apothecary. I believed the grown-ups thought we attended a far-out holiness tabernacle founded by an obscure apostle to the heathen.

In the summertime we did not have to go to Sunday School. Instead, we went to country churches near Birmingham. My father loved to visit with the rural people, and this was his most effective and enjoyable politicking. We children hated it. We wanted to stay with our fancy Birmingham friends, to go swimming at country clubs, to tell little dirty jokes under the bushes. We complained all the way out the highway and down the country lane, and as we sighted the church, my father would intone some quotation, like

> Let not ambition mock their useful toil
> Their homely joys, and destiny obscure;
> Nor Grandeur hear with a disdainful smile,
> The short and simple annals of the poor.
>
> The boast of heraldry, the pomp of pow'r.
> And all that beauty, all that wealth e'er gave,
> Awaits alike th' inevitable hour.
> The paths of glory lead but to the grave.

Though we did not fully understand him, that chastised and hushed us. We got out of the car and clung together like the little snobs we wanted to be, until a local kid picked a fight or caught a lizard or otherwise broke our ranks. Then we had a pretty good time.

Soon after we got there, the men set up sawhorses and planks under the pine trees in the churchyard, and the women spread out hams and beautiful black-brown hard-fried chicken. There were buckets of potato salad that had already begun to sweat before the cowbell called the eaters, and green beans cooked in side meat and kept warmish under brilliant homemade quilts. And purplish pink cakes with inch-thick goo and sometimes dates or peach slices embedded in them.

After lunch we all went in the little frame church with its tin roof and its two or three windows and the millions of flies lured by the pink cakes. In trembling voices the women sang old songs like "Give Me That Old Time Religion" and "I'm Going on a Honeymoon with Jesus." The local preacher took twenty minutes to tell God what a fine turnout there was and how the weather was just right. My father was always called upon for a few words, and he spent five minutes telling how he came to know the sire of this family and how this family was kin to a dozen other Jefferson County families, and five minutes discussing legislation pending before the Congress. Finally came a talk by the oldest, most feeble man in the family, listened to solely on the grounds of longevity, which for the poor, the Southern poor, provided the admiration great wealth bestowed elsewhere.

One of these old codgers—about eighty-five, the kind that is called spry because he walked jerky on stiff knees and looked like a cricket— got stuck on the phrase, "You eat sour grapes and you put your children's teeth on edge." At the start, the phrase seemed to punctuate his thoughts, but soon that was all he could say, over and over again, shriller and shriller: "You eat sour grapes and you put your children's teeth on edge, you eat sour grapes and you put your children's teeth on edge." He didn't even pause when he shoved his false teeth back in his mouth.

The church began to vibrate with that phrase. The children giggled and choked until the mothers sent them flying out of the building to fall howling in the dust. Finally, my father took the old man by the elbow and led him away from the pulpit, with the old man waving his arms and shouting, "You eat sour grapes and you put your children's teeth on edge." The grown-ups ran out of the church, jumped in their cars and drove away. That ended that reunion.

But the phrase lived on. For years after that, we Huddleston children chanted these words to express our rebellion against everything that we thought was simple-hearted and old-timey and dull. When we had to participate in the politicking, we marched to the tune of "You eat sour grapes and you put your children's teeth on edge." Although within a few years the family reunions and the Sunday

School-going both came to a close, we could always raise a pretty good family laugh by saying our favorite phrase.

As shocking as the Eagle Scout who murders his mother and father in their beds, after I graduated from college I went to the Divinity School of the University of Chicago. The Divinity School was hardly hard-shell or foot-washing Baptist, and the evangelist Billy Sunday had once dignified it by saying if you turned it over you would see "Made in Hell" stamped on its bottom. Nonetheless it was a divinity school, and my family and friends were struck dumb that I was going there. I had not been inside a church since my father quit forcing me to go, and ever since I first raised a ruckus at fourteen I had said I was not a Christian. So now why?

Very earnestly I said I found metaphysics and ethics the most worthwhile studies of all. I said that divinity school was literature, philosophy, history. I said that maybe I would find out that I really was very religious. At any rate, I had always thought a lot about dying.

But of course there was more than that. I had had a disheveled college career, achieving nothing, doing badly, until the religion professor got me interested in myth, evil, the historicity of Jesus. And I was a little in love with that professor. Also I was deeply disturbed by the racial situation in this country, and it seemed to me in those days, 1945, only the Communists and a few theologs gave a damn about blacks. It is also true that when I showed my free verse to an English professor, he suggested I try sonnets. Finally, I was striking out in a direction no one else in my family had ever ventured on. So I went to divinity school, unbaptized and Bibleless.

Although the intent was to undermine in the fashion of large, rowdy families, my brothers and sisters reinforced my calling. That summer my two brothers were home from the Second World War and were trying to adjust to everything that was different at home and everything that was the same. They did not know which I was. They watched me warily and used more profanity than usual until they saw I didn't care.

One night one of my brothers came in late, a little high on beer, drew up a chair to where I sat reading, and said in as confidential a tone as he had ever honored me with, "Okay, kid, you can trust me. What's your racket?"

"Man, God, and the Universe," I said benignly.

"Yeah," he said, "but I mean do you really believe that religion stuff?"

"Diothelite monophysite christology?" I asked.

"Well, sort of."

"Or do you mean," I went on, relishing the seconds, "that unlimited conceptual realization of the absolute wealth of potentiality?"

"The little Sunday School teacher," he said. "My, my, the little Christian."

When it was time for me to go off to Chicago that autumn, my brother and a law school friend of his named Arnold drove me to the train station. Arnold was a big good-looking debonair fellow who owned a pre-War Packard convertible and later became an FBI agent. On that ten-minute ride with the top down, he was clever and flirtatious and I was right taken with him. When he helped me out of the car at Terminal Station, he read aloud the title of the book I carried to read on the long train ride.

"*The Nature and Destiny of Man* by Reinhold Niebuhr."

We stood on the sidewalk appraising each other. "Niebuhr," he mused. "Niebuhr." And then his face lit up. "Hi, Niebuhr, what d'ya know and what d'ya say? Hi, Niebuhr, hi, Niebuhr." Right out there in front of the most public building in Birmingham, Alabama, Arnold and my brother commenced to do a soft-shoe dance and to sing to the tune of a popular song, "Hi, Neighbor."

"Hi, Niebuhr, hi, Niebuhr, get your chin off your chest, chase your troubles away. Hi, Niebuhr, hi, Niebuhr. . . ."

My sense of humor fell off me like a lobster's shell, and I was tender and vulnerable. I hissed, "Know-nothings, boobs, nihilists."

All the while laughing and shoving each other like little boys instead of the ex-naval officers they both were, they escorted me to the platform. As the train started up, Arnold yelled, "Bye, Niebuhr, bye Niebuhr, it's time to smile and say bye Niebuhr." With great dignity I donned my glasses and found my place in the book.

As the train left the station I was still smarting but reading along when two decent-looking, apparently lonely young sailors came to sit in the empty places in front of me. They leaned over the seat back, grinning, and one of them said, "How about reading aloud to us?"

I stared at him and I said, "All right, I will." And in a prissy nineteenth-century old maid's voice, I read aloud from *The Nature and Destiny of Man*. I had not read twenty-five words before the sailors were roaring down the aisle, whooping and hollering as if my drawers had fallen off. It was, I said to myself, the price I paid for being a theologian in an essentially frivolous world. Small price.

Nevertheless, when I got to the Divinity School, I felt less like a martyred theologian than like a hypocrite. I was pretty sure the faculty and other students didn't believe as I did. Or rather I was sure the others believed something—I was there to find out if there was anything I could believe. I kept to myself at the beginning, and in an effort to appear pious I didn't wear lipstick to class.

After a month or so, I discovered that all the bright theological students, and they were mostly bright, were playing an exciting game with the verities. They maneuvered metaphors and analogies as chess players shift queens and pawns. One group redid the Lord's Prayer in the language of the philosopher Alfred North Whitehead: "Our Process which art in the cosmos. . . ." And for me everything fell into place. I could do that. I could be a believer.

Fairly soon I could take the concept of the Trinity, in which I had never had the least interest, and polish it up with a metaphor or two and sell it to a heathen or a Jew. And think he ought to buy it, too. I could hook the Trinity onto Plato's the True, the Good, and the Beautiful (with the Holy Spirit playing the Beautiful) and who could deny it? The Virgin Birth, I said, was a statement in the language of myth attesting to the exceptional quality of Jesus. As we danced at the Trianon, at the Aragon, I asked my date if the Resurrection was anything more or less than the existential encounter at the bottom of the pit of despair. I accepted these metaphors as valid religion for our time.

I came to see, however, that the other young theologs played the game with a desperation I lacked. They had come more directly to divinity school from religious upbringings in devout homes. Before they doubted, they believed. After they shed their simple creeds, they felt alone and destitute. When they made their complicated "leaps of faith," they landed on somewhat familiar shores. They mocked, but they cared. The game they played was more than a game.

I wanted that more than a game, too. I wanted to believe in my seriousness, my conversion to the serious concern for the supreme good. During that eighteen-month period at Chicago, I spent a good deal of time thinking how absurd was human existence apart from a belief in God and a good deal of time thinking that there wasn't a thing I could do to remove that absurdity. For, despite my yearning after the wisdom of the theologians, from deep inside me there emerged regularly and as vigorous as ever the voice of the child who said, "I don't care."

After I got my master's degree in theology, I came back to live at my parents' house and to teach religion for a year at my old college. I was twenty-one, and half the class had been at Iwo Jima or at least Fort Dix, and among the other half was a sprinkling of ministerial students and old-timey Christians. I didn't know very much, and it seemed all I could do was stay a lecture ahead and try not to offend the true believers, who had a right to their serenity, yet not bore the ex-soldiers, who were required to take the course. Occasionally I became truly excited about some part of what I was teaching, like the problem of evil or the moral beauty of the Book of Amos. But I felt guilty at redefining important words and using them as if I believed them.

My religion, such as it was, such as it perhaps appeared to be, was constantly challenged by my brothers. And so I had to work to make religion intellectually respectable in our house. Hadn't I committed several years of my life to it?

"Well, goodness sakes alive," my brother said one evening when I was dressed for a date, "I thought you were going to be a nun."

"That's all right," I said. "You go on being content with the surface of life while I'm down in the pits mining the ultimates."

"Don't tease her," my father said. "It's good experience." The truth was he hadn't quite figured me out either.

One day a student of mine, a big gawk of a boy who wanted just enough education to be a backwoods preacher, came into the office I shared with the head of the Religion department. The boy wasn't doing very well, squeaking out a bare D, and I believe he came to talk with me out of a sincere desire for a better grade. He said, "Will you settle a quarrel for me? My grandma says God wrote the Ten

Commandments Hisself and give the tablets to Moses. I say God dictated and Moses wrote it all down. Which is right?"

I heard the head of the department snort, and I dared not look to him for help. That boy was as old as I and in lots of ways a good deal older, but in almost all ways simpler and more vulnerable. I thought of *Moses and Monotheism*, of all the legends parallel to this one, of the J and E and D sources of the *Old Testament* and the fact that *Exodus* told inconsistent stories of the tablets.

I said, "The important thing is that we have the Commandments, isn't it?"

The boy looked surprised and intrigued, and then he said, "That's right and we sure ought not be quarreling about it."

"Well done," said the department head when we were alone. He knew that kind of difficulty and how to evade it much better than I, for he doubled on Sundays as a minister. I accepted his "well done" as praise from an expert.

An hour or so after that, he swiveled his chair and said, "Would you like to take my pulpit one Sunday?" He had a queer smile on his face, with his lips rolled back over his teeth as though he was in the thrall of a wild adventure. I was pleased but uncertain, and so I fell back on earnestness.

"What Sunday did you have in mind?"

"Not next, but the one after. There's a conference in Nashville I'd like to go to." For a second longer he held tight to that queer smile, as if he were afraid it would break loose. Then he sobered. "I believe it would do my folks a lot of good to hear you. The new word on the old word." That put it in terms I could not resist, and I said I would do it.

At dinner that night, I told my family. My mother looked worried and fretful and said, "Do you think you should. . .a real church?"

My father, who looked on all of life as a training ground for perfection, said, "Of course she will: good experience."

"This is rich," said my brother. "I mean rich."

I worked on my sermon every evening for nearly two weeks. I titled it "The Sin of the Good People," which I copped from a Divinity School professor, though he shouldn't be blamed for the way I adapted the phrase. I wrote a paragraph or so on people who claimed to love God but obviously thought little of man, a few paragraphs on snubbing the poor and the black, on how churches grew fat and lazy and irrelevant, and I closed with the idea that the established churches were in danger of becoming social clubs.

Out of the Goodspeed Version of the Bible, which we had used as a text at Chicago, I chose two quotations. The one from *Matthew* read "If your brother wrongs you, go to him and show him his fault while you are alone with him. If he listens to you, you have won back your brother." The second reading was from *Jeremiah* 31:27: "Behold days are coming when I will make a new covenant with the house of Israel and with the house of Judah, not like the covenant I made with their fathers. I shall put my law within them and I shall write it on their hearts and all of them shall know me." My message was: Help is on the way.

The night before the service, I told my family I didn't want any of them present. My mother looked pained but accepted it. She was probably glad to avoid the suffering.

My father said, "Don't be ass-y. Of course I'm coming."

The church was a frame building badly in need of paint. It was on a busy highway, and I had caught it in transition between its rural past and its rich suburban future. When we drove up, a man recognized my father and drew him into a throng of churchgoers on the front stoop. I went in a side door, past the choir loft to a chair behind the pulpit. As the congregation gathered, I pressed my fingers together to hide my trembling and to appear thoughtful.

The choir director started off with a hymn and the 200 or so parishioners rose to sing. Then another song and then the First Reading. It took me a minute to find the chapter and verse of *Matthew* because the Bible on the lectern was the King James, and I couldn't easily recognize the passage. I heard my voice quavering as I read.

I had told the department head that I had never prayed aloud, and I asked him to get one of the church leaders to give the pastoral prayer. The church leader turned out to be my father's old political crony. He was a giant of a man with strong, slightly hunched farmer's shoulders and a gleaming red skull with a fringe of silver wire. He held his head high and closed his eyes and intoned, "Dear Lord, we thank Thee for this beautiful Sunday morning, for our good health, and the health of our loving families, and we thank Thee especially this day for sending to us to help us worship Thee this great congressman, this outstanding public servant, this fine citizen, this Christian man, George Huddleston, and his little daughter who gave her heart and her love to Gawd."

At that I tuned out, to nurse my bleeding heart and to dream of a fit torture for that man. When he finished praying I reared up, face hot, and charged the pulpit for the Second Reading. I flipped open the big old King James to *Jeremiah* 31:27 and read:

> Behold the days come, saith the Lord, that I will sow the house of Israel and the house of Judah with the seed of man, and with the seed of beast. And it shall come to pass, that like as I have watched over them, to pluck up, and to afflict; so will I watch over them, to build, and to plant, saith the Lord.

Throw down? destroy? afflict? seed of man, seed of beast? None of this made any sense to me in terms of my sermon, and I thought perhaps I had started the reading too early in the chapter. I decided to read on a bit.

> In those days they shall say no more, The fathers have eaten
> a sour grape, and the children's teeth are set on edge.

And our family marching song echoed through the church: You eat sour grapes and you put your children's teeth on edge. I looked up and out and across the congregation to the very back pew, saw for the first time the red head back there, stared straight into the blue eyes of my brother George. He gave first, his face shattering with held-in laughter. His hands flew to his mouth as he pretended to be coughing. Soon his face dropped below the pew in front of him, and all the air around jittered and quaked.

"Saith the Lord," I said and rushed back to my seat.

The pressure of laughter built up inside me. My eyes drowned in water, my throat and chest ached. I bit my knuckles, thoughtfully, trying to gain control of the volcano raging within me. I looked at my father, expecting him to chide me with a glance and settle me down as he had when as children we misbehaved in public. But he was quietly laughing, from time to time touching his fingers to his lips to settle himself down. A soprano in the choir loft belted out a sturdy tremolo, and then it was time for my sermon.

I thought I couldn't do it. I saw that never for a moment during all those years had I had any real religion. All I had was a mighty fear of dying. Theolog: me? What a laugh. It was clear to me that I shouldn't have accepted the invitation to preach. I shouldn't be teaching religion. I shouldn't have gone to divinity school. You go against your real nature, bend it or deny it wholly, and it's bound to end badly. I didn't know whether to cry or to laugh, but I was perfectly certain that I would do one or the other if I tried to speak.

I stood up. Maybe my family never had any real religion, but we always had a sense of responsibility to the feelings of society. And we always took pride in ourselves. These were part of my nature, too. My father stopped laughing, adjusted his body the better to listen, and casually nodded encouragement. He never doubted for a second that I would do my duty to all the middle-class folk of Christendom. I snuck a look at George. He, too, had straightened up and grown solemn.

My heart was not in that sermon. It took all my concentration just to stay sober and pretend to be serious. But as dozens snored, I read my way through the pages, got past all the innumerable faults of the good people to where I extended to them a bit of hope for salvation. I made it. I got to the end. And after the service, I stood at the back of the church to receive gratitude and admiration for having given my heart and my love to Gawd.

George and my father waited by my car. As I approached, they watched me closely to see how well I had survived. I punched my father on the shoulder and said, "It's all your fault. You're the one ate all those sour grapes." The three of us laughed and sighed at the truth of that.

The Birthday Party

FOR OUR FAMILY, my father's birthday was the big occasion. It was a drama enacted over and over again, with variations, for nearly twenty years, until my father was close to ninety and could no longer enjoy his starring role. All five of us children always made a point of being there, even those who moved away from Birmingham. But we were at best stagehands or ticket-takers. My mother and father were the stars and the old men who came were the supporting cast.

Every party was a near-tragedy. My father would always disrupt the plans at the last minute, and my mother would always become agitated and almost always furious. She was twenty-two years younger than he, as social as he was private, as impulsive as he was thoughtful. We sometimes said he had married her for her high spirits and spent the next forty years trying to curb them, and she had married him for his reserve and dignity and spent the next forty years trying to get him to change.

The birthday parties began when my father turned seventy. On a late October evening, after he had gone to bed early, as he always did, my mother said, "Two weeks and your father will be seventy. No one would believe it—he looks so young." She stopped her quick crocheting fingers. "I worry about him, though. He just stays home all the time. He never sees anyone."

When my father was defeated for the House of Representatives after twenty-two years and we moved back to Birmingham, he had withdrawn from public life. He went downtown only once a week, and he almost never visited with old friends. He tended his affairs in his little home office, visited his country property, read, and played solitaire. Though only in her forties and still volatile and feisty, my mother tried to conform to his way of life. She spent her days knitting, crocheting, piecing beautiful quilts. She had a few friends she visited with, and for entertainment and gaiety, she had her children and her children's friends. Though the sharp edge of their life never wore smooth, they eroded a bit during their last years together.

She smiled at us. "What if we had a birthday party for him?"

"He'd have a hissy," I said.

"He probably wouldn't even come," said my brother.

"Well, then, we'll have a surprise party," my mother said. "We won't tell him and when the guests show up, he'll just have to behave."

"Hohoho," I said, and my brother said, "A surprise! God. Can't you just see him."

My mother shook her head. "He pretends to think social doings are silly, but he'll like it once it happens. He misses seeing people, really, down under."

"Australia's down under," my sister said, "and it's mostly desert." We all laughed.

"Laugh, clowns, laugh," my mother said. "You'll see I'm right."

And so she decided on the party. She wrote my sister, the only one of us then married, to come home for the party, and my sister said she would, if only to see the fireworks. My mother asked our cook to find two people to help with serving. She counted the dishes and had the silver polished. Then she began on the guestlist.

"Just his old friends," she said. "No women."

"That's silly, just men," my sister said.

"Men like to get away from their wives every once in a while," she answered. "Just men. Just old friends. Let's say if he hasn't known them for thirty years, they can't come. Except the boys."

The boys were my brothers.

"Of course the *boys* will be there," I said in my most sarcastic voice. "That's only right and proper."

"Men at the table. Women in the kitchen," my brother said. He was a good-natured but teasing fellow, and he loved to get a rise out of me. He knew how irate I could become when the boys were treated differently. For us girls, equality was a constant struggle in the family. When I had turned sixteen, my father said that I didn't really need to learn to drive a car because he would guarantee that my brothers would take me anywhere I wanted to go. My brother had teased me about that and I became so wild with fury that I stole his Model A Ford and, not knowing how to drive, had coasted down the hill as far as I could and landed part way up a stranger's driveway. That episode was still fresh in our minds.

"Not this woman in the kitchen," I said. "If I'm not invited, then I'm not helping."

"I'll certainly do everything *I* can to help," my brother said in a playfully self-righteous voice.

"This isn't the dark ages," my sister said.

"No, it isn't the dark ages," my mother said with her eyes on her list, "but it is my house and my party, and I want my sons to get to know these old friends of your father's. If you don't want to help, don't." Thus did she effectively quell our rebellion.

She began to write down the names of the guests. "Doctor Horton. Remember when you broke your big toe," she said to my sister, "and he gave it such a twist to set it that you shrieked like an alley cat?"

"Cats don't shriek because their toe gets broken," my brother said. We all laughed.

"You needn't teach me the facts of life," my mother said. "I believe I know enough without your help. Mr. Blake. Back in the old days, he used to drive your father out to Gintown and around there, and then he'd wait around during the speech. Judge Clancy. Your father was best man in his wedding over forty years ago."

And on and on she went, making affectionate comments after each name, until she had a list of eleven old friends.

The next day she telephoned the guests. "It's to be a real surprise," she said. "He doesn't know a thing about it."

Then she decided on a menu. First they would start with orange blossom cocktails.

"Give 'em gin, give 'em bourbon," my brother said. "That's what the old boozers want."

"No, I want it to be nice," she said. And then the truth came out: "I can make up the cocktails early in the day and just add ice, so no one will have to tend to the bar. And for dinner we'll have Robbie's wonderful fried chicken so your father won't have to do the carving. And green beans cooked in fat back."

"Cooked to death so that not a vitamin is left," I said.

"These old men don't want vitamins," she responded. "They want good food. Onions in cream. Wild rice with mushrooms. Sweet potatoes. Black cherry salad. Hot biscuits. Pecan pie. And champagne, of course. Lots of champagne. A dinner fit for a king."

"Greasy beans and champagne," my brother said, shaking his head and laughing. "Now that's a combination."

"You don't have to eat it," Mother said in her quick way. "That would mean more for everybody else."

During the days just before the party, my father grew irritated because the maid was always disturbing him, washing windows even though he was trying to nap on the sofa, dusting right under his nose, concealing his things, his cards, his books, so he couldn't lay a finger on anything.

"Do we have to clean house every day?" he said. "Is this some new-fangled fetish of your mother's?"

My mother realized that on the last day my father would find out about the party because of all the bustling about, the extra help, the last minute errands. ("Is someone giving away gasoline at the corner?" he would no doubt ask.) She decided to ask a close friend, Mr. Blake, who knew how ornery my father could be, to invite my father to lunch on the pretext of needing advice.

"And that way he'll have on decent clothes," I said.

His untidiness had rankled all of us ever since he had closed his office and said, "From now on I dress any way I wish." What he wished was to wear my brothers' cast-off clothing and a pair of houseslippers. What he wished was to shave twice a week and to have his hair cut by anyone who happened to be standing nearby. When at first we refused to cut his hair, he cut his own. The only time he put on a suit and tie was for his weekly trip downtown.

"Otherwise he'll just look like a derelict," my sister said.

Mother said, "Quit being so critical. He doesn't care what people wear."

"Well, I do," I said.

"Then you should spend your energy making yourself look as beautiful as possible," she said in her quick voice.

The morning of the party, my father shaved and put on his best white shirt and one good suit and the black bowtie he usually wore. He left the house at eleven-thirty.

Mr. Blake kept my father talking about a real estate deal until midafternoon. After a quick trip to the bank and the safe deposit box, my father went to catch the bus for home. One of the guests, forgetting that the party was a surprise, came up to him and said, "I'll see you at your party tonight."

When my father arrived home he flung back the front door so that it crashed against the wall. "What's the big idea?" he shouted when my mother came to investigate the disturbance.

"Yes, dear?" my mother said.

"So," he said, "you thought you could put something over on me. Am I not to be consulted over how I am to spend my own birthday? This is outrageous."

"It's just a party," my mother said. "It isn't a revolution or an earthquake." He ignored her.

"I might as well tell you now," he said, "when your secret little guests come, I won't be at your silly party."

My mother stared at him and her face turned red. "You're the most ungrateful person in the world. No one can do anything nice for you."

"How could you deceive me," he said, "and make me a laughing stock? It was all Sam Blake could do not to laugh in my face. A secret. A little surprise party for little children. Well, I'm not senile yet. Your guests may be childish enough to come, but I won't be there."

When all the roaring and stomping had begun, the whole house started to quiver. The cook peered around the kitchen door and quickly withdrew. My sisters and I went quietly to our rooms and shut the doors. Why should we offer ourselves as sacrificial lambs?

62

But when his thundering voice reached its peak, we decided to brave his wrath and come to stand up for our mother. "Come on, now," my sister quietly said to him.

"You're being foolish," I murmured, hoping the words would reach home but hoping their source would be lost.

When he saw that we were arrayed against him, he looked at us bitterly and said, "A birthday party for an old man. Talk about female nincompoopery, and all of you in it."

He went into his office and began to shuffle papers.

In the kitchen my mother let her anger turn to tears. She had a good cry while we patted her shoulder and talked loud and hard about what we would do if we had a husband like that. My married sister said, "I would never allow my husband to behave that way." My mother shot her a look.

"I hope he isn't as boring as you make him sound," she said. "I hope he has some gumption." She looked around at the pots and pans. "Let's see, what should we do next? I don't care whether he comes or not, I'm having a party."

As the time of the party approached, my sisters and I wanted to find out what our father would really do. And so each in turn, we entered the living room, where he was playing solitaire, and walked slowly around him trying to get up the nerve to ask him. Finally he said, "You act like a covey of vultures circling carrion."

"Well?" my sister finally managed to ask.

"Well what?" He started laying out a new hand, all the while eyeing her through his brows. "What kind of a question is 'Well'?"

She squared her shoulders and plunged on. "I want to know if you are coming to the party or are you going to humiliate Mother?"

He stopped dealing, and stared at her. "So the Furies have decided that I'm humiliating her. She hasn't humiliated me at all, has she? The solidarity of females."

He threw his cards on the table, watched with satisfaction as they slithered to the floor, and then stalked out of the house. We saw him marching toward the bus stop.

When my brothers arrived, Mother said, "Well, it looks as though you boys are the hosts."

"You've got to be kidding," one of them said. "I don't even know most of these old geezers."

"Men at the table," I said, in an innocent voice. "Isn't that the way it's supposed to be?"

He turned on me. "You're such suffragette, you should be dying to take over."

Before I could point out that I was both willing and able, Mother cleared her throat, signaling us that she had had enough of the wrangling.

When the guests arrived, my brothers led them into the living room and received the presents, the bottles of scotch and the flamboyant unwearable neckties perhaps rescued from the bottom of a drawer. Soon, however, the old men began to fidget, with no host to play to and breathing the unfestive air.

"Where's the old boy?" asked Judge Clancy. "Did he refuse to attend his own party? I wouldn't be surprised."

"He's just a little slow getting dressed," my brother said. The conversation stumbled on.

My sisters and I roamed the back quarters of the house, moving a chair a fraction of an inch or bending a flower in the centerpiece. We listened intently for a door to open, a miracle to happen. The cook shook her head and went on cooking.

My mother was in the kitchen, too, mumbling. "I'm not going to beg him," she said to no one. "If he wants to act like a child, let him. It'll still be a nice party."

She stared out the window, and then she wrapped a sweater around her shoulders and slipped out the side door. My sisters and I went to the window. We could see him across the street in the shadow of a large elm. He looked like a sentry. We saw our mother go up to him and put her hand on his arm.

"Can't you just hear her?" my sister said indignantly. "'I'm sorry. I should have consulted you. I'm sorry. Please come in.'" We saw her take his hand and tug at him and coax him back across the street.

And so they became friends again, or at least no longer foes, occupying the fluid middle ground that marked the major portion of their life together. Relief and irritation sighed through us. How could she? Thank God she did.

When he joined the old men in the living room, he said, "Gentlemen, welcome to my birthday party. This is probably my last birthday and I'm delighted to have all my old friends celebrate it with me."

Mother said, "Isn't he foolish? He'll be here until he's a hundred." She beamed at the genial host.

And so the party began, with orange blossom cocktails that the old men eyed suspiciously and recollections of old times. Soon my mother appeared and nodded to my father. He stood up.

"Gentlemen," he said and motioned them to march into the feast. They set upon the food ravenously, as old men seem to do. And they washed it down with great quantities of champagne. My mother kept insisting that everyone eat everything and eat more of it. My sisters and I replenished the dishes and served the men—and the boys. Soon the talk rose again.

My father was at his most jovial, telling old political yarns. "When we used to go politicking out in the country," he said, "Sam here packed a pistol, stuck it right in his belt."

"I never," said Mr. Blake.

"Maybe never used it," my father said, and everyone laughed.

"Well, somebody had to look after you," Mr. Blake answered. "You were too scrawny to look after yourself." And the old men laughed again.

The guests began to leave at ten o'clock. With each departure, my father said, "I thank you for coming."

When the last guest left, the whole family was in the living room. My father looked at us but did not look at my mother. "It's past my bedtime," he finally said, and then went up the stairs without another word.

We began to clear away the brandy and water glasses and return the chairs to their proper stations.

My mother said, "Well, now, that was a very successful party."

"You had to eat a little crow," I pointed out.

"That crow didn't taste too bad," my mother said. "I hope you never eat worse. Your father really had a good time. And wasn't he a wonderful host?"

"He didn't say a word of thanks," my brother said. "I'd be mad as hell, if I were you."

"Isn't it good you're not me, then?" she said. "I know he's appreciative. You children just don't understand him."

She sat down and seemed to be ruminating. Finally she said, "When we have the party next year. . . ."

We five children sitting in that room stared at each other in outraged disbelief. And then we groaned and laughed so loud that she couldn't tell us her plans for the next year's birthday party.

The Man Who Said No

MY FATHER WAS DEFEATED for Congress in 1936, after serving for twenty-two years. He lost in a blaze of notoriety. He had gone back to Birmingham to politick for the May Democratic primary—the only election that counted there in those days. Usually he only campaigned for two weeks and spent no more than twenty-five or fifty dollars on cards and broadsides. But this time he knew he was in for a tough election, and so he spent a month in Alabama and two or three hundred dollars for radio time.

School was still in session in Washington, and since he had school-age children, he left the family there. One morning about a week before the election, my mother sent me to the front porch to get the *Washington Post*. When I opened the newspaper, searching for the comics, our name flew up at me. The headline read, KETCHUP BOTTLE DUEL IS VICTORY FOR HUDDLESTON.

I ran to show my mother. Her face went from white to red to white again, like a lightbulb going off and on. "Something terrible must be wrong with him," she whispered. Violence and impulse were so foreign to my father's nature that she was sure he had had a nervous breakdown.

She telephoned to the hotel where he stayed when he was alone in Birmingham. "I haven't lost my mind," he said, "only my temper. The fool's not hurt. In fact he's pleased as punch." He said he had not telephoned us because he didn't think the event would be reported

67

outside Birmingham. In fact, it was reported in every newspaper in the country.

He said he had been eating dinner in his usual restaurant when his opponent accosted him, stuck a finger in his face, and in a loud voice accused him of lying in a radio address. My father had picked up the ketchup bottle on the table and cracked it down on the man's straw boater.

When I got to school that day, my sixth grade classmates clustered around me, some to comfort, some to jeer. I didn't much care which. I felt downright famous and I strutted around the school yard all day. Those were the days of Joe Louis, another Alabamian, and I remember thinking, George Huddleston, the White Bomber.

By that evening, my mother had calmed down. When she noticed how I swaggered, she took me aside to set me straight. She said the episode was hardly anything to be proud of. She said my father was terribly ashamed of losing his temper. She said it probably meant his seat in Congress.

I said, "He didn't want to run anyway."

"That's right," she said, "but nobody wants to be defeated."

His opponent in the election was a lawyer turned radio announcer. He gave advice to his listeners and read homely quotations and corny poems. Though my father said he was just a buffoon, the man had quite a following among radio listeners. More important, he had the active support of the Roosevelt people in Birmingham, the mayor, the postmaster, the Alabama head of the mine workers, and Senator Hugo Black. He also had the support of all the enemies my father had picked up over twenty-two years in office, including the leadership of the Ku Klux Klan.

Although smashing his opponent's straw hat did not help, most people said my father lost because he had shifted his politics. When he had started his political career, he had been called a radical, even a rabble rouser. Now he was called a reactionary, a sycophant of the rich and powerful. He had sold out, they said, to the very interests he had fought throughout his career. He scoffed at the idea and thought it indicated shameful ignorance.

By the standards of today, and maybe any day, my father made an odd politician. He was small and rather shy and introverted. There was nothing hail fellow about him. He seldom complimented and never flattered. He was too proud to lie or trim. He considered it his duty not to compromise just to please the voters. In fact, he seemed happiest when he opposed the crowd.

He had been born in Tennessee a few years after the Civil War, and his family had lost everything in Reconstruction. He went only to the third grade of a country school and then became a butcher boy on a train, hawking sandwiches and candy. In his twenties he started law school, and when he graduated he moved to Birmingham. He rented a desk in another lawyer's office and slept on top of the desk. According to an account book we found after his death, he made thirty-seven dollars his first year and a hundred and eighteen the second.

He began to concentrate on bankruptcy law during the hard times of the 1890s, and he soon developed a thriving practice. Within a few years, however, he came to believe his clients were mostly crooks, hiding assets from their creditors and the courts and him. He was in his early forties and a bachelor, and he had enough savings to live, and so he quit the law. After a year in Europe looking at pictures and cathedrals, he came back to Birmingham and ran first for alderman and then for Congress.

Though raw and young, Birmingham was rapidly becoming the industrial center of the South, aided by a tremendous influx of Eastern capital. It had all the natural ingredients necessary to manufacture steel—limestone, iron ore, coal, and cheap labor, white and black. An enormous steel plant owned by the United States Steel Corporation, now USX, dominated the economic and political life of the city. Effective labor unions were twenty years in the future, and the workers had little power.

As a lawyer, my father had hobnobbed with the established people of Birmingham: businessmen, bankers, other lawyers. But when he became an alderman, he befriended the working people. He helped to change the form of the city government to stop domination by the powerful few. He agitated for control of the smoke nuisance of the coke ovens and the piling of waste slag in poor neighborhoods. He opposed a sales tax, saying that it would be "levied upon poverty and not upon wealth." At a time when most Southerners were rabid racists, he made a speech to the Alabama Legislature saying that the franchise must inevitably be extended to blacks.

He took on US Steel and the other absentee owners of Birmingham's industries and banks. Absentee ownership meant that the wealth Birmingham produced largely went east. He believed that the protective tariff had reduced the income and increased costs of Southern farmers and workers. Eastern big finance and big business, he thought, deliberately kept the South in poverty and dependence.

Despite the opposition of most of what in Birmingham were called "the got rocks," he was easily elected. He went to Washington in 1915. Woodrow Wilson was President and the First World War had started. My father was appointed to the Foreign Affairs Committee of the House. He seems to have had a knack for placing himself at the center of the storm: he shifted his focus to the Interstate and Foreign Commerce Committee in the 1930s, in time for the domestic battles of the New Deal.

Along with a handful of other representatives, he believed that the country was moving toward war. He said that a powerful coterie of militarists "have laid their plans for vast armies and navies, on universal conscription for cheap soldiers, and to teach the people servility and obedience." He blamed the growing American imperialism on Eastern financial and business interests.

He had been a volunteer in the Spanish-American War, but he had come to believe that Admiral Dewey steamed into Manila Bay so that big business might seize "the Philippines as a base for expansion in China and the Orient." And though the Panama Canal was widely hailed as an immense American achievement, he criticized what the United States had done to achieve it and said that "we raped Colombia [once the legal government of the Isthmus of Panama] so that we might extend our operations throughout South America." In speech after speech he spoke scathingly of the Union League Club in New York, of such men as Cornelius Vanderbilt, Elihu Root, and Joseph H. Choate. He called these men "the natural enemies of democracy."

As a newcomer, my father would probably have gone unnoticed in Washington except for his oratorical gift. Though restrained and quiet in person, he was aggressive in public speech. He seemed to compensate for his small size by a large, bass voice and for his reticence with a ready and sarcastic wit. He could smoothly shift from bombast to subtlety, from ridicule to sentimentality. He could be both self-righteous and humorous. He had schooled himself in literature, and he was not afraid of the high-flown phrase and the metaphor. Though he seldom won a following on an issue, he seems always to have had an appreciative audience.

A major issue that engaged and enraged him—and which caused him to break with Wilson, his Party's own President—was conscription. He believed that peacetime conscription was a giant step toward war and toward tyranny. In one speech, he asked, "Where does the support for this odious system come from?" And of course answered his own question:

> The military system, with its manifold gradations, with its iron discipline which has as its ideal the making of a senseless human machine with which the superior can work his absolute will. . . .
>
> The great financiers. Owners of railroads and ships; captains of industry, . . .who would send the American flag into remote corners of the world so that rich profits may be brought home to their coffers.
>
> War traffickers, munitions makers, builders of ships for the Navy and contractors of Army supplies. Those who coin their profits out of human blood and suffering. . . .
>
> The parasite press. The corrupt newspapers preaching the doctrine of reaction; subsidized by selfish interests; echoers of all the undemocratic voices in our country. . . .

When the German government declared that it would begin unrestricted submarine warfare, and began to sink American vessels, United States involvement became inevitable, and my father, albeit with grave reservations, supported the declaration of war in April 1917. Yet he still believed that conscription was evil. Perhaps not quite ingenuously, he said that conscription was "an imputation against the courage and patriotism of our people" and that since "property is not so sacred in its nature as life and liberty," the country ought first to conscript property. After conscription became the law, he proposed that officers and conscripted enlisted men receive the exact same pay and the same pension.

As it had drifted toward war, the country had become more and more xenophobic. There was a great outcry against German-American citizens, and anyone who opposed the war was called a traitor. At Wilson's behest, the Congress passed an Espionage Act in 1917 and made it even more stringent in 1918, broadening the definition of espionage to include any obstruction of the war effort, including speech. My father opposed both acts, saying they were "a more drastic restriction on liberty than any measure ever before passed by Congress even in time of war."

And he continued to assail big business and to call for increased taxation of war profits. He said that "no man has the right to grow rich out of this war." He claimed that the war profiteers, among whom he classed his congressional district's largest employer, US Steel, were parasites:

> Swollen with insolence and egotism, [the war profiteer] seeks to dominate the life of the community. He gives of his spoils to war charities enough to make himself respectable to his own dull conscience and to that of others of his class and then seizes if possible, some conspicious position in connection with war work and assumes to be an authority on public duty. He hectors labor, bullies the timid and "strong arms" such modest citizens as he can intimidate, and woe be to all those who may expose him or seek to tax the proceeds of his extortion. . . . He stands with his right hand in the public pocket and with his left hand flings mud at anybody interfering with his game.

These and like words hardly endeared him to the got rocks back home. More important, by the time of the election of 1918, he had alienated President Wilson.

The publisher of Birmingham's major newspaper, a long time opponent of my father's, had been a classmate of Wilson's at Princeton. He apparently persuaded Wilson to break the unwritten law of politics that the leader of the party does not campaign in the primaries against a member of his own party. However it was arranged, Wilson telegraphed the newspaper saying that "Mr. Huddleston's record proves him in every way an opponent to the administration."

The newspaper published the telegram on the front page and the other newspapers picked it up. The next day a caricature of my father appeared in the morning paper. It showed him with a big head and a little body encased in jodhpurs and leather boots. A hammer and sickle were emblazoned across his chest. The caption read "The Little Bolshevik."

For several days after that, caricatures appeared in all the Birmingham dailies. He was depicted as the protector of a German anarchist, as a pygmy trying to hold back a giant Wilson, as an anarchist overturning the Statue of Liberty.

He was not then or ever had been a member of the Communist Party or an anarchist or even a left-leaning socialist. He was a nineteenth century liberal, with beliefs he called Jeffersonian. Individual liberty was the supreme good. The Bill of Rights must be strictly interpreted, including the tenth, or states rights, Amendment. Centralized federal authority was a great threat to democracy. Bigness itself was evil. These were his most cherished beliefs.

The night after the cartoon appeared, his supporters organized a rally in the city park near the center of downtown. My father and mother, who had married a year earlier, were coming into Birmingham on a train. According to a sworn affadavit, albeit from a supporter of my father, the railroad tracks had been soaped in order to delay their arrival until after the rally. But the word that the got rocks were after him had apparently spread among the farmers and coal miners and steel workers in the outlying districts, and though the train was three hours late, over fifteen thousand supporters bearing lighted torches jammed into the park and spilled onto the downtown streets.

After he won the election, more easily than he had expected with such potent opposition, my father decided to sue the newspaper for libel. He brought the suit in a rural county in his district because he thought he could get a fairer trial from a jury of farmers than from people who might be under the sway of the got rocks. He won the suit and was awarded $30,000, a fairly large judgment for those days. The newspaper appealed and the case went to the Alabama Supreme Court, where the newspaper had more influence than it did in Oneonta, Alabama. The decision was overturned on the grounds that the suit should have been brought in Birmingham because that was the primary site of publication of the libel.

(Forty-five years later this decision became part of *Sullivan vs. The New York Times*. During the civil rights upheaval, a Montgomery, Alabama city commissioner named Sullivan objected to the way the *New York Times* reported his part in events and sued for libel. Not surprisingly the Alabama court found for him, and the Alabama Supreme Court upheld the decision. On appeal to the federal court, the *New York Times* lawyers referred to *Huddleston vs The Age Herald* and suggested that perhaps the Alabama court hadn't read its own law, because obviously the primary site of publication of the *New York Times* was not Montgomery, Alabama. The *Times* won that case, though not because of this facetious reference.)

My father did not sue again, perhaps because he didn't think he could win in Birmingham. He settled for a front page retraction and apology. After that apology the newspaper always referred to my father as "the incumbent," "the congressman," or "Birmingham's representative." It did not mention the name George Huddleston again for fifteen years.

After the War, the country took a sharp turn to the right. The War had led to even greater concentrations of wealth and power and more conservative, even reactionary, politics. Republicans took over the presidency and the Congress. The corporations were riding high.

Although he apparently had little support from his fellow congressmen, my father continued to speak as a "radical" throughout the 1920s. He claimed that the federal government had intervened in a miners' strike not to keep the peace but "to intimidate the miners and drive them back to work." He tied this event to a federal raid on a meeting of the Communist Labor Party in New York. He said the real purpose of the raid was:

> ... to intimidate workers as a class. It was to strike terror in the heart of every foreigner in this country and to make him feel. . . that he dare not take part in a strike for fear he would be sent back to some bloody land where his life would be forfeited."

When Republican congressmen accused him of creating unrest by this speech, he responded, "Communists are not made by words; socialists are not made by words. They are made by the overpowering eloquence of situations, of injustice, and of persecution."

During the Twenties, United States business rapidly expanded into foreign markets, particularly in South America. As business expanded, so did the "national interest" of the United States. My father opposed this new imperialism as he had that of the turn of the century. He suggested that business interests were fostering war with Mexico "for the profits they hope to derive from the new 'conquest' of Mexico," and that these interests had controlled the State Department completely when "Mr. Charles Evans Hughes, attorney for the Standard Oil interests, was Secretary of State." When Marines were sent into Nicaragua, my father said Coolidge had intervened not to protect American lives, as the President had claimed, but

> . . . for the purpose of establishing the particular government that happens to be satisfactory to him and to those behind him. . . . (Nicaragua) has lost its independence. It is now for practical purposes merely an American possession. . . . What we are doing in Nicaragua today we are bound in good faith to do in every other Central and South American country tomorrow— unless we are afraid—unless they are too strong. . . . Great Britain in her most arrogant days never dreamed of an imperialism to that extent; imperial Rome never asserted over other powers any comparable authority.

A Republican in the House pointed out that Wilson had coerced Mexico in similar circumstances. My father responded that he had condemned Wilson for it, and said, "I will not withhold my condemnation from the immeasurably smaller and weaker man who now happens to occupy the presidential chair."

When the Great Depression struck, my father turned from foreign affairs to domestic ones. He was the second ranking Democrat on the Interstate and Foreign Commerce Committee, after Sam Rayburn who had beat him to the House by one month back in 1915.

Within a year of the stock market crash, unemployment was running as high as 40 percent in some areas. My father blamed not capitalism itself, but a corruption brought on by "combinations, trusts, monopolies, and conspiracies in restraint of trade." He said the country was "reaping the harvest of the collectivism" sown by the Republicans. With their favors to special interest groups, they had encouraged extortionate profits that brought on inflation and depression.

When the Hoover Administration introduced a public works bill, my father scoffed that it was intended to help those least in need of help. He said 40 percent would go to business for overhead, profits, and salaries, and the remaining 60 percent would go to the most "intelligent, strong, and able-bodied" laboring people, likely to have savings accounts and other means to endure the depression. None, he said, would find its way to "the decrepit, the infirm, and the crippled, and none to those who have no skill and no training." The people most in need of help would be left to starve.

And so he introduced the first bill calling for direct government relief. He said that such a proposal was not inconsistent with individualism, that all governments, including the United States since 1804, had attempted to relieve the suffering of the people. When the Hoover Administration objected to direct relief, my father said, "We have a man in charge who is more interested in the pocketbooks of the rich than he is in the bellies of the poor."

During the Twenties and early Thirties, he was often re-elected without opposition. Though Southern and conservative, laboring and farming people supported him enthusiastically. They were proud that a man who had means, position, and learning, and could have counted himself among the got rocks, was on their side.

He was not always on their side, however. Though the voters of Birmingham, almost all of English descent, were hostile toward Jews and other new immigrants, he opposed laws that would curb immigration. He defended Tom Mooney, a wartime labor agitator convicted of murder, and other men he thought persecuted because of their politics. When so many of the men of his district joined the Ku Klux Klan during its resurgence in the mid-Twenties, he was almost alone among Alabama politicians in opposition. His life was threatened by Klan leaders, and steel workers and coal miners—including Klansmen—volunteered to serve as his bodyguards at political rallies. When his constituents overwhelmingly supported a federal prohibition amendment, he voted against it because he said it violated the tenth amendment to the constitution, the states rights amendment. And later when they wanted to repeal prohibition, he voted against repeal, because he said the method proposed was itself a violation of states rights. It never bothered him that some called this apparent contradiction perversity.

The voters did not expect him to think exactly as they did or to follow them. They allowed him a freedom of thought and expression that would infuriate voters today. They did not consider a congressman a clearing house of popular opinion but rather a leader. They were proud of his independence, even from them.

Once Congress adjourned for the summer, our family always went to Birmingham. This was the time of my father's most effective politicking. We rented a large house and there my father had his office. Each weekday, a flood of people came asking for help. The widow of a veteran might need help in getting a pension. A citizen might have a cousin in Ireland or Germany he wanted to bring over. One might seek a job as postmaster in one of the hamlets—the only patronage my father had. Another might simply want advice on some marital or business problem.

On Saturdays he often took us to reunions of families not our own. Even when I was only six or eight years old, I could tell how proud the people were to have him there. Men would crowd around him and slap their thighs over every joke he made. Women would shyly bring up a son or a daughter to shake his hand. Often there were contests at these reunions, potato races and hog callings and prettiest cake. And my father was usually the judge.

On Sundays we often attended the little churches in the outlying towns and villages. And he would preach the sermon. He did not pretend to be a believing man, but he put his oratorical gifts to work on the rights of labor and the glories of farming, and he got his share of Amen, brother, amen. After church, our family would take Sunday dinner with a parishioner, and in the afternoons the people of the neighborhood would drop by to pay respects.

We Huddleston children often objected to these outings. We preferred to hang around with our fancy country club friends and tell Little Audrey stories. We found hog calling an embarrassment. We liked cold milk from bottles, not warm milk from cows. We thought the children talked funny, and on the way home we sometimes imitated their "nahce brot lot" for "nice bright light" and their "ain't" and "we come."

My father would say, "Quit posturing." And then he would intone a favorite poem of his:

Princes and lords may flourish, or may fade;
A breath can make them, as a breath has made;
But a bold peasantry, their country's pride,
When once destroyed, can never be supplied.

Despite the obvious element of paternalism in his attitude, he deeply respected his constituents. He admired the hard-muscled miners with the lines of their faces never quite shed of coal dust and the farmers whose gait was always slightly tilted from working the hill country. He thought they represented the virtues on which America had been founded: resoluteness, fairness, hard work. But he also thought he knew what was best for them and for the country. For twenty years they, too, believed he knew best.

And then, with the New Deal and the great economic changes of the Thirties and the shift of political power, there came the parting of the ways.

When Franklin D. Roosevelt took office in 1933, my father thought that at last he would have a leader he could follow, and he was an avid supporter. He thought Roosevelt believed in pretty much the same ideas he believed in, that Roosevelt was a Jeffersonian liberal. Such, it turned out, was not the case.

One of Roosevelt's first proposals was the National Industrial Recovery Act. As Richard Hofstadter says in *The American Political Tradition*, "in essence the NRA embodied the conception of many business men that recovery was to be sought through systematic monopolization, high prices, and low production." The NRA promoted an economics of scarcity and central control. In 1935, the Supreme Court ruled it unconstitutional. But it was symptomatic of the New Deal: the Administration would create a new economic order. The government would help to control the economy in order to limit the ravages of free enterprise.

My father opposed the NRA and most of the subsequent Roosevelt economic measures. He blamed the country's economic ills not on the free enterprise system itself but on a corruption of it: protective tariffs and trade barriers that inhibited foreign trade and increased prices, trusts and monopolies encouraged by government privilege, excessive profits caused by the decline of competition and the concentration of wealth, deficit spending, and, at the heart of it all, federal infringement on states rights. He thought that a government-planned economy, and restriction of free enterprise, would hinder recovery and that centralized control presented a grave threat to individual liberty. As the ranking Democrat on the Interstate and Foreign Commerce Committee, of which Sam Rayburn was the chairman, my father tried to dam the flood of government intervention in the economic life of the people and the states.

There was another factor in his opposition, a psychological one. He was what in those days was called an "aginer." He had entered the Congress opposing one popular Democratic President and here he was opposing another. He had obviously become accustomed to being an "aginer," and he enjoyed the role. He began a speech on a bill that he thought would allow a monopoly of bus transportation with:

> I rise in my accustomed role as objector. . . . Some of my friends tease me and say, "Oh yes, you are against everything." Of course it is useless to deny and so I plead by way of avoidance, "Yes I am; and the trouble about it is I am always right." I have sometimes thought that a Member might come into the Chamber and without knowing what was going on vote "no," "no," "no," on every proposal and his batting average would be about 900.

He said a "no" vote was apt to be right because when committees were writing legislation the "interests" were always there lobbying, but the people were never represented.

Perhaps he had a David complex, if such exists. A Southerner, an autodidact, an undersized man, he loved to go forth to do verbal battle and to sling his words at the Goliaths of business and politics. And so he began his political career opposing one Democratic president and ended it opposing another.

Things were different back home this time. The labor leaders, grown stronger with Roosevelt, fully supported the New Deal. When my father opposed the NRA, they turned against him. In 1934, they put up a candidate who would go along with Roosevelt. The election was the closest of any my father had ever had. He won that one, but he thought he would probably not win the next—he had offended too many people. He said he didn't want to run again, but he thought it was important for someone to say the things he said.

The newspaper he had sued had become part of the Scripps-Howard chain and vigorously supported the New Deal. The paper now mentioned my father's name, but again disparagingly. Its Washington columnists claimed that "George Huddleston... despite loud protestations of devotion to the cause of liberalism, has waged bitter war, usually behind the scenes, on some of the President's key reforms." Though the complaint was the same—Huddleston did not support the Administration—the expression was different. My father was no longer "The Little Bolshevik"—he had become the darling of Wall Street.

He did not believe he had changed. He thought the nation had whirled past him on a crazy, destructive course. He could not accept that the nineteenth century principles were no longer applicable. He did not believe that the terms in which he viewed politics and economics—states rights, individual liberty, competition—were obsolete. He held to his Jeffersonian beliefs while, he thought, the country was becoming dangerously centralized and the government authoritarian.

In the summer of 1935, his opposition to the New Deal came to a head with the Holding Company Bill. The ostensible purpose of the bill was to regulate the utilities, but the effect of one of its clauses, called "The Death Sentence," would be to abolish utilities holding companies. My father had for a long time favored regulating them as he believed in vigorously regulating and restricting all trusts and monopolies. He objected, however, to destruction, claiming that it would punish innocent stockholders and interfere with free enterprise. If the Congress wanted to punish the perpetrators of the holding company misdeeds committed during the "economic orgy" of the Twenties, he said, "you would have to pursue them into the Great Beyond, and I would suggest you clothe yourselves with asbestos." He claimed that the Death Sentence put too much power into the federal government and violated the spirit of the Constitution.

When his good friend Sam Rayburn deserted the House version, which did not contain the Death Sentence, in favor of the Administration/Senate version, my father said, "He abandoned his new-born child and walked off with the Senate jade." To no one's surprise, least of all my father's, the Senate version passed the House.

The columnist Arthur Krock reports in his *Memoirs* that soon after the passage of this bill he was at Joseph Kennedy's and heard Roosevelt and some of his assistants singing, "Old George Huddleston ain't what he uster be, ain't what he uster be."

A few months later came the ketchup bottle incident. The only other time my father acted violently that we ever knew about was forty years earlier when he had been similarly insulted by the opposing lawyer after a heated trial. The two had exchanged threats in the courthouse and then deliberately misaimed pistol shots at each other as they passed on the dirt streets of the bristling wild young town of Birmingham, no harm done. Perhaps here again he felt his honor had to be defended.

Or perhaps he was raging against his imminent defeat. He knew it was coming—if he squeaked by this time, he would lose the next. Nobody wants to be defeated, my mother had said. She might have added, politicians least of all. Judging by the reaction of politicians I have known, defeat in an election must feel like a personal rebuff. Although the voters think they are merely expressing difference of opinion on the issues, politicians seem to think their very being is the issue. When the voters reject the candidate, they reject the personality and character of the person. Anger and humiliation seem the occupational hazards of politics.

We moved back to Birmingham in 1937. My father thought he was too old, 68, and rusty to practice law again. The utilities companies did not come forth with a juicy job, though during the election his opponents had implied they surely would. Birmingham did get the new government building, rumored to be the reward the Administration offered.

My father became a semi-recluse. He seemed to view his career as a failure, despite the twenty-two years in Congress and all those overwhelming elections, despite the exultation and pride he felt in battling the rich and powerful and popular, despite standing firm against the strong winds of change, despite the fact that if he wasn't "what he uster be," he at least once had been. Though vigorously urged to run again because of the growing anti-Roosevelt mood following the Court-packing attempt and the third term, he refused. He refused to make speeches or go to meetings or even express his opinion on the issues. Now he wanted nothing to do with the people of Birmingham who had elected in his stead an Administration rubber stamp and buffoon. He was finished with politics.

Once an acquaintance stopped him on a downtown Birmingham street and said, "Well, I had to vote against you this time because you'd just gotten out of touch with the world."

My father said, "That's your right."

Perhaps trying to be friendly, the man said, "How does it feel to be out of office after so long?"

My father said, "It feels good to be able to tell people like you to go to hell," and walked off.

He turned his mind to the country property he owned near Birmingham. He drove out to the property and walked through the beautiful woods, whacking through the underbrush with a cane he carried. When he finally hired a man to put in a few roads, he rode along in the cabin of the bulldozer. Once a week he went downtown to the bank, the broker, the real estate agent, and lunch with a few old friends. And he read and he played solitaire. That was the life of this man who had been at the center of so many great debates.

When my brother was elected to my father's old seat twenty years later, my father, then in his middle eighties, gave him some advice. He said, "If you want to get along, go along." But when Alabama's cotton industry was suffering from foreign competition and a move was afoot to increase the tariff on cotton, my father wrote to my brother telling him it was his duty to vote against the evils of protection. My brother received over fifteen hundred letters from his constituents favoring an increased tariff and only two against. He was not by nature an "aginer," but I'm happy to say that on this issue he voted No.

My father died in 1960, in his ninety-first year. In its obituary, the newspaper he had sued in 1918 commented that "his records defy all efforts to catalogue him."